Words of Wisdom
from Women
to Watch

Words of Wisdom from Women to Watch

Career Reflections from Leaders in the Commercial Insurance Industry

Business Insurance

Published by John Wiley & Sons, Inc., Hoboken, New Jersey.
Published simultaneously in Canada.

For general information on our other products and services or for technical support, please contact our Customer Care Department within the United States at (800) 762-2974, outside the United States at (317) 572-3993 or fax (317) 572-4002.

Wiley publishes in a variety of print and electronic formats and by print-on-demand. Some material included with standard print versions of this book may not be included in e-books or in print-on-demand. If this book refers to media such as a CD or DVD that is not included in the version you purchased, you may download this material at http://booksupport.wiley.com. For more information about Wiley products, visit www.wiley.com.

Library of Congress Cataloging-in-Publication Data:

ISBN 9781119341499 (Hardcover)
ISBN 9781119341505 (ePDF)
ISBN 9781119341512 (ePub)

Printed in the United States of America
10 9 8 7 6 5 4 3 2 1

To Dave North, CEO of Sedgwick, for his steadfast advocacy of gender equality and enduring support of the Business Insurance Women to Watch program.

To Kathryn McIntyre, Business Insurance's former publisher and editor, whose "Salute to the Top 100 Women" in the year 2000 served as the inspiration for Women to Watch. In fact, many of the women recognized at that event, held on October 10, 2000, at the Fairmont Hotel in Chicago, were later named Women to Watch honorees.

To all women executives worldwide in the insurance/reinsurance, brokerage, benefits, risk management, and related fields. You are all Women to Watch, preparing the way for others who follow.

Contents

Foreword

Joanne Wojcik
Head of Event Programming
Business Insurance magazine

R ecognizing that the commercial insurance industry was—and still is—a largely male-dominated field, *Business Insurance* magazine launched the Women to Watch Awards in 2006 to identify and shed a spotlight on those women who have the potential to become its future leaders.

Each year, a panel of *Business Insurance* senior editors selects 25 honorees from hundreds of nominations submitted by readers based on recent notable professional achievements, their influence over the industry and marketplace, and their own contributions to the advancement of women. The editors also tried to imagine what likely next steps these already successful women might take to further their careers.

For a decade, the profiles of these Women to Watch honorees were published in a December issue of *Business Insurance,* and awards were presented at a ceremony held annually in New York City. *Business Insurance* added an educational component to the program in 2011 with the introduction of a Leadership Workshop featuring many alumni of this elite group of female industry professionals. In 2014, this event was expanded into a full-day conference intended to further foster women's progress by identifying the challenges they face and offering advice and actionable solutions. The conference was open to both men and women who support achieving true gender parity among the senior ranks of the commercial insurance industry and related fields.

The year 2015 marked the 10th anniversary of this unique recognition program, and *Business Insurance* held an evening gala to fete that year's honorees. In addition, *Business Insurance* recognized three prior-year honorees for their continuing contributions to the advancement of women in the insurance industry: 2008 honoree Bonnie Boone, senior vice president at Marsh USA, who launched a networking group for women of color; 2006 honoree Corbette Doyle, lecturer of leadership, policy, and organizations at Vanderbilt University, for her research into the influence of women serving on corporate boards; and 2006 honoree Inga Beale, who in 2014 became the first female CEO of Lloyd's of London, a 350-year-old institution that didn't even admit women until the 1970s.

As we have seen from the women we have profiled in this annual feature over the past decade, the pool of talented and dynamic female executives holding key positions within the sector is growing and will continue to flourish as barriers to women's advancement are removed. Unfortunately, there still are not yet enough women at the top levels of management in the commercial insurance industry to represent the diversity of the workforce coming in. In fact, while more than half of entry-level positions in the insurance industry are held by women, just 12 percent of senior managers are women, and only 1 percent of the CEOs in insurance are women.

This book, which features a collection of essays by several past Women to Watch honorees, is a tribute to those women who have broken through the proverbial "glass ceiling" in the commercial insurance industry and are continuing to battle for gender parity among its executive ranks. Women's advancement in this and other industries is not just a "women's issue"; it is an economic imperative. In order to have a competitive workforce and a robust global economy, companies need to leverage the full potential of all of their talent—both women and men.

Having more women in leadership positions also is good for business. It's not that one gender has any greater ability than the other; it is that a more diverse group makes for better decision making and corporate performance. A recent study by Credit Suisse Research found that companies with higher female representation at the board level or among senior management have better financial performance and higher stock market valuations. Moreover, the more female board members there were, the better the companies performed. Those whose boards included at least 25 percent women delivered a 22.8 percent greater annualized return than those with no female representation. Another study by Catalyst found that companies with the highest number of female executives outperform those with the fewest number of women executives, yielding a 26 percent greater return on invested capital and 16 percent more in sales.

Given the small number of women currently in the high-level roles in the insurance industry, men are a crucial part of the equation. The fact is, when male leaders participate in gender diversity initiatives, they are far more successful than they would be otherwise. Research by McKinsey & Co. identified three key attributes shared by organizations that have made significant strides toward achieving gender diversity:

- First, companies with more women on the board in 2007 had more women in top leadership positions in 2011.
- Second, industries that attract more women, such as health care, are more likely to have more women in top leadership positions.
- And last, but certainly not least, when the CEO demonstrates a personal interest in cultivating gender diversity through both speech and actions, the organization tends to have more women in leadership positions.

It is for that reason that *Business Insurance*—and all of the Women to Watch who have been recognized—owe special thanks to Dave North, the CEO of Sedgwick, for the publishing of this book. It was his vision that the Women to Watch not only be recognized, but heard. He thought that by giving them the opportunity to share their personal experiences and the lessons they have learned, they might make the journey easier for those women following in their wake.

By sharing "words of wisdom" from past *Business Insurance* Women to Watch honorees, this book is intended to inspire all women who are looking to advance their careers or who would benefit from hearing their peers' personal perspectives. The book addresses the various issues and obstacles that historically have affected women's careers—such as childbearing, achieving work-life balance, or breaking through the glass ceiling—while also offering some advice and direction.

"The day will come when men will recognize woman as his peer, not only at the fireside, but in councils of the nation. Then, and not until then, will there be the perfect comradeship, the ideal union between the sexes that shall result in the highest development of the race."

—*Susan B. Anthony*

Acknowledgments

This collection of stories represents not only the women who contributed them, but also everyone in our industry who has supported the progress made in gender equality over the years. These advancements have been driven by industry leaders such as Sedgwick. Without their passionate commitment to the intrinsic value the female perspective brings to every facet of our business, our industry could not have achieved so much in the last three decades. This book is a tribute to all of the women and men who cherish the unique talents and experience each individual contributes to the whole. May this momentum continue!

Words of Wisdom
from Women
to Watch

Chapter 1

I'm Strong

Ingrid Lindberg
Customer Experience Officer
Chief Customer
http://chiefcustomer.com/

Building the Framework of Steel

I was a little girl who loved to wear tutus and play in the mud with my army figurines. Growing up on military bases around the world, I was encouraged to be strong. All of my authority figures were strong. From my dad, who was in charge, to the Military Police who surrounded us every day, to my mother who packed up our lives every 18 to 36 months and moved us across the world. They were mentally and physically strong.

In addition to that military influence, my father was an attorney and my mother was a teacher; coupled with an outstanding vocabulary, I learned to joust effortlessly at the dinner table. Having strong opinions that you could back up with facts was a requirement. I was encouraged to participate in the discussions with the adults; a children's table did not exist.

My mother's favorite story to tell about me is when she picked me up from on my first day at Montessori school. Apparently, the directress (Montessori's version of a principal) approached her at pickup time. My mother's recollection of the conversation is as follows:

Directress: "Are you Ingrid's mom?"
Mom: "I am."
Directress: "Well, apparently, I don't need to be here any longer, as your daughter is definitely in charge."
Mom: "Why? What did she do?"
Directress: "Because she's telling everyone what to do and every-one is listening to her."

I was 18 months old.

They pushed me. They celebrated my accomplishments. They expected me to do well. I remember being in fifth grade. I was the only girl who sat in the "smart kids" row in our math class. My teacher, Ms. Andrade, would keep me after class and encourage me to raise my hand, to speak my mind. She told me that I had to be smart and strong.

I remember working my way through advanced placement classes in high school and being one of the only girls there. Girls were dropping like flies. It wasn't cool to be smart. I kept on.

When I was 14, my world was rocked. My parents got divorced, and because we needed the money, I started answering phones at a salon and making appointments. I worked there almost every day after school until they closed at 9 P.M. Then I'd have to go home and do my homework, which taught me about a whole new type of strength.

Through college I worked multiple jobs, including managing large retail stores. I learned how to balance classes and life and run a business. I led some of the most successful branches of several national retailers. Despite all the successes, there were lessons about strength there, too. I'll never forget the day that a district manager walked into our store, after a double-digit increase in sales year over year, and the only thing she had to say to me was that my skirt was too short. I was 20 years old. I began to dress differently, and I was angry about it. It was the first time I had run into someone asking me to change because I didn't fit their expectation about how I should look or act.

When I walked into Corporate America at 24, I was a strong, confident, intelligent woman who didn't understand hierarchy. I understood that rules were important for order, but I didn't have any fear when it came to pointing out what could be done better.

My first Corporate America role was as a trading agent in a contact center that placed trades for 401(k)s. Six weeks into that job, I found myself standing in the chief information officer's office one night telling him about all the changes I thought we should make to our platform. I laid out all my points, with supporting facts and solutions. He asked me who I was, but he didn't tell me that, according to the rules, I wasn't supposed to be bringing these recommendations directly to him.

He ended up listening to me, and we implemented many of the changes I'd suggested. He was my first big supporter. Because of that platform, I was afforded the opportunity to work with many of the giants in financial services. My career path was fast and furious, and I rose through the ranks quickly.

Again, that success was dotted with challenges that made me stronger. I experienced so much blatant sexism that it actually became a part of my strength. I wore higher-necked shirts. I stopped wearing skirts. I wore less makeup. I thought that was the way to stop it. I was called "Missy" and "Honey." I spent years reminding men I worked with that my eyes were higher than my breasts.

I've been asked if it is "that time of the month." I had a leader ask me if I'd "taken my pills" that day. Later, that same leader, at an event for which I'd been asked to give the keynote speech, said to the person who had arranged the entire event that his job was to "babysit Ingrid and make sure she stays out of trouble."

And I kept on responding to all of this with humor and strength. We weren't encouraged to report things like that—after all, "boys will be boys." I was told to toughen up.

I got stronger.

The Fraternity

Fraternities are important. They create inclusion. They protect. They are for people of shared interest to create communities. They are supportive.

However, they also foster exclusion. Corporate America has been built around the support of the fraternity, from the places where "deals are done" to the business that is done over brown liquor and cigars. The fraternity that was built to help men get from one stage to another is one that seems impenetrable for women.

Fraternity is built with people who are like you. "The human tendency to gravitate to people like oneself leads powerful men to sponsor and advocate for other men when leadership opportunities arise."[1]

Whether the ticket to entry was a shared love of golf, fishing, or some other activity that I have no interest in or time for, I've always been stymied by the fraternity. I've tried to crack it. I've learned how to tell jokes. I can order, and enjoy, scotch. I've been known to smoke a cigar. I've been encouraged to be tougher, be more like the boys—learn to play with the boys. I've been told that I should spend more time after work hanging out with the guys. Literally, all words of wisdom I've heard.

Fraternities have built a certain kind of toxic business environment of insiders and exclusion. I questioned the assumption that I should try to join.

What I find most fascinating is I've been rewarded for learning to drink brown liquor and hang with the boys. I've been held up as evidence that a woman can successfully navigate a male-dominated company or industry. On the other side of this, I've watched senior women be fired for drinking too much and "misbehaving," yet I've never seen that happen to a male executive.

I once had a person walk up to me at an event, very late in the evening, and tell me, in front of many of our peers, that he liked to "get nekked." For real. That underneath his suit was a "wild and crazy guy." He then asked me if I'd like to go back to our hotel with him.

A friend of mine witnessed this. He offered to walk me back to our hotel. We escaped. The behavior was explained away by this group

---

[1]https://hbr.org/2013/09/women-rising-the-unseen-barriers

of men, saying that he was just "having too much fun!" and they laughed about it for years. His behavior was excused because he was part of the fraternity.

We're Not Helping Each Other

I was employed in a senior role at one company, and it was suggested to me that I meet with one of the most senior women in human resources. She was one of the only other women on the executive team, and she was incredibly powerful. I was told she'd be a phenomenal mentor.

I'll never forget my meeting with her. I set up some time based on her schedule, but clearly I wasn't a priority—as a new, young, female executive. She kept moving our appointment time and time again. This went on for months.

Finally, almost a quarter later, we both found ourselves at an offsite board meeting. I approached her later in the day, after we'd both completed our presentations. I sat down and we started chatting. It was all very amiable. At one point I paused, and with a significant amount of deference in my tone asked her for advice on navigating the company. It was a high school boy's locker room for sure. . . . I commented on how successful she had clearly been at doing so, and I asked her if she'd be willing to work with me.

She paused and said, "No one helped me. Why should I help you?"

I'd asked for help and been denied. It was a moment of having to find a whole new layer of inner strength. I decided at that moment that it was up to me to do something to change the game, to try and make sure that no one else received that same answer.

Years later, I read an article that described what I'd experienced: second-generation bias. One of the components of second-generation bias is the bidirectional feeling that there is limited worth. That means that younger women may have a bias against older women in the workplace—that they may not be the people to go to for networking, career help, and so on, and that older women may have a bias against the upcoming generation.

That whole notion of "No one helped me. Why should I help you?"

I refused to believe that was an appropriate response. I have made it my mission to help younger women. As word spread, I had a constant stream of requests for mentoring. It got to the point that I had to structure my weeks with very specific rules. There were only so many hours that I could spend with women who were in search of guidance—in and outside of work. One happy hour a week, two lunches.

Still, I knew I wasn't helping everyone that I could, so I started creating informal women's networks. I'd connect women who were more senior and with a mentoring mind-set with women who were newer in their careers. I opened up a night a month to a women's happy hour where women from all sorts of industries came together for networking opportunities. Women formed bonds. Women gave and received advice. Women shared and created job opportunities for other women.

I worked at another company where I asked the senior human resources leader if I could start a women's network. She told me that she didn't think that was a good idea. After all, if we organized women, other groups would organize, too. I did it anyway. It was underground, but I created it.

I have continued to create those networks, both formally and informally, at every company I have worked for.

I'll never forget the day I left one firm. The announcement went out, and I was stunned by how many e-mails I received. There were thousands. The woman in charge of my life, my executive assistant, made copies of several of them for me. The two piles that were important were the ones from people she knew were important to me. The other pile, from women who I'd never met, writing to tell me that they'd seen me speak in an all-employee meeting, or that they'd heard about how I'd helped a friend of a friend and how I was a role model to them. That they felt more confident in their ability to speak up because of me. There were hundreds of those. I still have that pile of printed e-mails.

My Children, or Lack Thereof

In my 20s and 30s, I was asked time and time again why I didn't have children. It started as such an innocent thing, I think. Many of the women around me, if not most, had children. Younger women, older women—they all had elected to have kids. It was almost as if I were looked down upon for having made the decision not to have children.

I was asked this question by colleagues and associates so many times that my answer became so ingrained, it was an extension of my personal elevator pitch. "I loved playing with Legos and Lincoln Logs when I was a kid. I never had any baby dolls that I carried around, pretending to be mommy. Motherhood was never a calling for me, but I'm so glad that it is for you!" Huge, bright smile on my face.

As I got older, the questions became more hushed. People actually had the audacity to ask me if we'd been trying but were unsuccessful. Were we not able? Quickly followed by some heartwarming story of a friend or family member who had success with in vitro fertilization or my favorite, "When they stopped trying so hard, it just happened!"

The first time that happened, I was stunned. Really. Stunned into silence. It was one of the first times in my life I didn't have a retort. How do you respond to that? My "I loved playing with Legos" line didn't work. The voice running through my head told me that it wasn't appropriate to say, "I have no desire to have children."

No one seemed to ask my male counterparts that question.

Then there was the year that I was told I was the highest-rated and best performer, but that my bonus wasn't going to be as big as I thought it would be because my boss needed to ensure that the bonus dollars were spread around—because my male peers had families.

I got stronger.

Mansplaining

If I had a dollar for every time I was interrupted, I'd be retired by now. Then add to that "mansplaining," and I'd be retired and supporting all my friends and family. My friends and I have had this conversation for years. And it still happens. Every. Single. Day.

According to Merriam-Webster: "*Mansplaining* is, at its core, a very specific thing. It's what occurs when a man talks condescendingly to someone (especially a woman) about something he has incomplete knowledge of, with the mistaken assumption that he knows more about it than the person he's talking to does."

One of my favorite mansplaining stories is from a panel I was on. (We could talk for days about the underrepresentation of women on panels and as speakers at conferences, but I digress. . . .) I was on this panel, the only woman, representing a topic that I'm an expert on. I was there as the expert, and the other panelists were all experts, too—albeit in other topics.

I was asked a question by the moderator, which I answered. I tried to be brief, as I always try to ensure that all panelists get their respective air time. One of my fellow panelists, however, decided that he needed to add on to my comments.

I'll reiterate: although an expert in *his* field, he is not an expert in *my* field.

In an exceptionally condescending tone, he corrected my comments about the "right" way to approach a problem, droning on using phrases like "I'm sure Ingrid meant to say . . ." and "In my vast experience, I've approached this problem this way. . . ."

That strong person inside of me just couldn't let it go. I allowed him to finish and then proceeded to challenge and correct every statement he had made, using facts, not opinions. When I finished, the audience burst into spontaneous applause. At our next break, I was surrounded by both men and women, congratulating me on stopping the mansplaining from someone who clearly wasn't an expert but clearly did like to hear himself speak.

Physical Size and My Love of Shoes

I'm short. I'll admit it. I have a posse of friends who love to remind me that at 5′6″, I'm actually pretty tall for a woman, but at the tables I'm usually at, I'm definitely the shortest. I always wished that I was taller. I wanted to be one of those women who could look eye to eye with someone in a conversation. The average height of women in America is 5′4″, and the average height of men is 5′9.5″. Yup—they even get the extra .5 inch.[2]

I'll tell you from my experience (validated by Malcolm Gladwell[3]) that executives are taller than that. The average male CEO is just a hair under six feet.

---

[2]www.livestrong.com
[3]http://gladwell.com/blink/why-do-we-love-tall-men/

The thing about size is that it gets used as a weapon of intimidation. I was having a conversation with a man who was junior to me in rank but taller than I by at least eight inches. I was telling this gentleman that although I understood his needs, my team wouldn't be supporting his request. I explained why he wasn't entitled to this specific set of perks, partially because of rank (I know, so old school), and he was becoming more and more frustrated.

As his frustration rose, so did he. Until he was towering over me (I was still seated), using his physical stature to physically intimidate me into doing what he wanted. I remained seated during this entire exchange, and after a few minutes of being spoken down to, I told him to "sit the f*ck down."

Now, no, this was not my most tactful response, but it was one that was merited in that moment. Luckily, he did sit down. I told him we could continue the conversation when he was calmer, but we never did.

Unfortunately, this isn't the only time I've experienced this. Knowingly or not, size is used as an intimidation method, so my strength was built up as to how to verbally respond. I learned to be very pointed in those moments because they happened so often.

My other counter to this size issue was to amass an outstanding shoe collection. I learned pretty early how to walk in four-inch heels. I lived in them for years. It made it much easier to at least get closer to eye level. I'll pay for it for years (in bills to my podiatrist), but the ability to not have to look up at a male peer, or be "looked down on" by one, was worth it.

Reviews

I have every single performance review document I've received since my first "corporate" role. Twenty of them. There are two consistent themes as I look back on all of them.

Those themes are: "Highest Performer" (or some version of that) and "Strong." What is interesting about those two is that in most of the reviews, it is acknowledged that the performance was accomplished because of the strength.

Despite this, I've received feedback that's as confusing as it is conflicting. Almost without fail, from both female and male leaders, this feedback followed a series of advice that included a level of "please tone down the strength." Some examples:

"Develop more caring relationships."
"Have more empathy."
"Show others that she cares about them."

What I find disturbing about these comments is that, over the years, I've also been told repeatedly to stop being so soft, to be stronger, to toughen up. What I find fascinating is that every time I've had to complete some version of executive profiling, I've always come out points and points ahead of "where I'm supposed to land" in empathy.

Years ago, for example, I was going through the hiring process for a very senior change agent role at a new firm. The firm had a required executive assessment that its candidates went through. It was a two-day, in-person, exceptionally intensive interview process with a series of psychologists, PhDs, and behaviorists. After the two days, a robust report was produced, and as a result of that report, you were deemed either fit or unfit for the role.

One of the tools in this packet was the CPI, the California Psychological Inventory–Executives. The layman's description of this tool is that it takes the participant and ranks him or her against the "norms" for executive personality types across multiple behavioral traits. I matched pretty much data point for data point, with the exception of empathy. My empathy was 10 points higher than the norm. Yet, it was listed as a possible derailer.

When I saw this result, I asked myself: Is it a derailer because you view my empathy as weakness, or is it an asset that I don't exhibit enough of? The fine line that women are expected to walk between being strong and empathetic is exhausting.

Strength Is Suddenly a Weakness

Although performance reviews were littered with mixed messages, I was lucky for many years in my career to be supported by people who loved how strong I was. They encouraged me to speak, to act, to drive ideas and change. They were men and women. They were my direct leaders, they were peers. They were CEOs, COOs.

Then, suddenly, something changed. I found myself in a climate where I wasn't supposed to speak up, and if I did, I needed to do so in a way that didn't upset my peers. They felt uncomfortable when I was strong. Better yet, I was supposed to "be less strong and more gentle."

You've read my years of stories. You've watched my strength be built.

I've sat at executive tables where the "F" bomb is used in place of "the." I've had people scream at the top of their lungs near or at me. I've had men throw attaché bags (lovingly referred to as a "murse") at me.

I'd been told my entire career to toughen up, so I couldn't quite comprehend how to take this new advice about my strength and the need to be "gentle." So I ignored it. I kept on being strong. I got things done. I had extraordinarily loyal employees. I had tons of accolades.

Eventually, I was mandated a coach because I was too strong. My coach told me that I needed to add "grace" to my strength. That I needed to be more thoughtful when I was contributing, that I should lower my voice. I couldn't quite understand why it was I, not them, who needed to change. But I wasn't given a choice. I was one of very few women on the executive team, and, clearly, the expectations for my behavior were different than for the men.

At first, I was asked to read several books. One of them had a passage in that still, to this day, infuriates me:

> Society expects women to be small, sweet, and quiet while using their time to make themselves pretty. Women are also expected to be perfect mothers or mother figures. When women fight against these basic expectations, by taking higher powered jobs or choosing not to have children, they are often attacked and made to feel as though they are failing in some way. It is this that is the source of shame for most women.[4]

Seriously. Shame? Shame for being strong enough to be leaders and follow our own paths? Shame for being successful? What have we

---

[4]Brené Brown, *Daring Greatly* (New York: Avery, 2012).

done when we're being told we have shame that we're carrying for being strong and successful? It's a message that went against everything I believe about the benefits of being strong.

I was completely honest with my coach. I didn't want to change. It felt like I was being stripped of the strength and uniqueness that I built through every interaction, every win, every loss. I was being asked to become a different human being. She was honest in return. "Try it their way *and* start looking for a new job."

I tried to do it their way. I stopped talking at the table. I stopped contributing. I stopped being me. And I was miserable. My leader was overjoyed. He couldn't stop gushing about how much I'd changed. What a pleasure it was to work with me now! The transformation!

So I left. Because I was silenced. Because I was not able to be me. The strong woman who spoke her mind, encouraged or not, was buried. She who was celebrated and promoted and awarded for all of her strength and her ideas had been silenced.

We're So Far from Done

What I have learned is that we still have a tremendous amount of work to do. Until we can change the corporate culture of "strong" being a negative for women yet a positive for men,[5] think of all the ideas that are being silenced. We must be a part of the change to create equality with the terminology of what is a celebratory adjective for men and a derogatory one for women.

Look at the reviews you write—are you penalizing your female employees for being strong while telling your male employees to be stronger? I've done it. I'll bet you have, too. Stop it. Look at your team. Are your leaders doing it? Stop that, too.

Work to change the way that performance reviews are written at your company. Set up searches for words that we know are disproportionately used with a negative connotation and flag them before reviews are given. Offer training to teach leaders about their bias.

---

[5]http://fortune.com/2014/08/26/performance-review-gender-bias/

We need to make *bossy* as positive a word as *leader.* Tell your little girls that they are exhibiting outstanding leadership skills, don't call them bossy. Or help them understand that bossy can be a good thing.

We need to stop trying to make women into exceptionally strong, but never intimidating, superhumans.

The tight rope between "one of the boys" and "soft like a lady" is untenable. Just imagine for a moment if every man were told that they needed to be softer, less abrasive, and more like a woman in their performance reviews. Perhaps that is an experiment we should run.

We need to stop encouraging women to "lean in" and instead encourage men to "reach out."

I have been blessed with many men who did reach out. They saw me struggling with less supportive leaders and ensured that they bolstered me. Formalize it. Create more formal and informal mentorship opportunities between senior men and emerging female leaders. Teach the men about the bias we face.

We can find leaders who will support our strength. We can find leaders who will support us and help us grow. Most importantly, we can create situations where we aren't trying to change people into a vision of what we think they should be. And that starts with us.

If you see a woman being subjected to mansplaining, or being interrupted, stand up for one another in those moments. When you see it happening, stop it. When you are watching a counterpart experience it, speak up. And if it is happening to you, point it out. You must.

One thing is for certain: We have to talk about it even though it is an uncomfortable topic. I feel like I'm sticking my neck out—and that is scary. And most importantly, as women leaders, we cannot be a part of it. We have to stop the cycle of second-generation bias.

I'm doing it for my goddaughter and my nieces because I want them to be celebrated for their strength, not penalized for it. I'm doing it for the thousands of women I've been lucky enough to meet in my career who have experienced these things and more. Speak up for your daughters, wives, nieces, or sisters. Do it because it is the right thing to do.

And I'm committed to talking about it because I want to be able to be celebrated for who I am, that strong little girl who loved to play in the mud in her tutus who turned into a strong woman who knows she can succeed at anything she sets her mind to.

Chapter 2

My College-Self Says, "What Glass Ceiling?"... My Now-Self Responds

Lindsey Frase
Executive Vice President
Willis Re, Inc.

A t 22, life feels pretty rich. Angst ridden, maybe. Full of promise, absolutely. Beginning my senior year at Santa Clara University in 2002, Beyonce was still part of Destiny's Child, and my Seattle Mariners had just won 116 games. Roughly half of the students in my undergrad business classes were female, and the honors business group to which I belonged had a gender-similar distribution. While there were only 13 females in the U.S. Senate (13 percent) and a paltry three female CEOs in the Fortune 500 (1.4 percent), this concept of the "glass ceiling" was categorically not a problem of *my* generation. What glass ceiling?

Surely, we were past it. Given my own life observations and experiences, it seemed clear that the strong and capable women of the prior generation had already fought that profoundly important battle. Sure, we hadn't had a female president yet, and executive ranks weren't quite 50-50, but I knew with that senior-in-college certainty that we were basically "there." My generation didn't need to fight to play sports (thanks, Title IX) or to get a higher education. My class photo would look nothing like my father's law school graduation picture proudly framed in his office. I recall time and time again as a child counting the women in the picture. It was (always) three. I remember that vividly because it was so remarkably foreign to my own experience. Thankfully, that wasn't going to be a problem for me—that battle had been fought and won. When I graduated at the end of that year, I would enjoy entering a mostly gender-equal workforce. Neither I nor my other female classmates had any reason not to expect parity in treatment, opportunity, and pay.

Fast-forward to 2013.

At this point, I had been working as a reinsurance broker for 10 years, experiencing great opportunities navigating a still decidedly male industry and largely balking at anyone who suggested that the path to the top was more difficult for women. But as I was promoted to executive vice president, I could count on a single hand the other female EVPs at our firm (a title whose ranks number around 100 globally). This fact very literally caused me pause. I began to rethink my staunch position that all of these "issues" were behind us. I started thinking about it differently and, frankly, just paying a bit closer attention. In 2013, there were 20 female senators (20 percent) and 22 female CEOs of Fortune 500 companies (4 percent). That was progress from my halcyon college days, but frankly, it is pretty pitiful. What happened to 50 percent? I began to realize that the issue hadn't quite been as effectively resolved as I might have assumed. I recalled the words of one female client, which I had ignored as irrelevant, realizing they may be more accurate than I previously cared to admit: I needed to fight for other women, advocate more, and very simply recognize that this issue was indeed still an issue for *my* generation. Because while I had assumed we were past it, the reality is, we really aren't. I hope that this message reaches others, and that my contemporaries take up what we all felt was a cause for our mothers' generation. Moreover, the issue of parity isn't limited to gender, and efforts should be made toward broad inclusivity around gender, race, and ethnicity, among other things. While my comments are focused on my own experiences as a female in business, there are certainly parallels that I hope will resonate more broadly for diversity in general.

I summarize some actionable considerations on how each individual can help to take on that notion of a glass ceiling and be an advocate for women (and other underrepresented groups) in the business environment:

Demonstrate...

...not just your aptitude but your intention to excel and your unwillingness to take an unsupportable "No" for an answer. You are likely capable of doing the job, of making the pitch, of contributing to the team.

From the very beginning of one's career, I have found that clearly demonstrating excellence will catapult you quickly forward. Demonstrate eagerness for new opportunities and ask to be involved on new projects, to do more work. We have all heard time and time again of research saying young girls are less likely to raise their hands in class or speak up at a meeting. How can your excellence be recognized if you do not speak up? Here, particularly if this is an area of comfort for you, encourage others who are less eager to share their views. Open the door for someone else to make her voice heard. It is also well documented that women feel more confident speaking as experts, with considerable data or experience substantiating a point, while men are generally happy to opine extemporaneously. Embrace this approach and find areas in which to hone your expertise so that you may demonstrate it categorically. Yes, it will take some additional legwork (and a little foresight), but embrace it as an investment in your career, your future, your ability to demonstrate excellence and be invaluable.

Elevate...

...your game. Walk in and own the room, because if you don't, someone else will, and, frankly, you are probably pretty impressive.

I have often noted that the most successful women (and men) in the insurance industry have a strong executive presence. They command attention simply by exuding confidence. Some things are cosmetic and fairly easy, like a firm handshake, eye contact, and being the most smartly dressed person in the room. Never match the lowest common denominator—if anyone is in a suit, wear a suit. This is oddly more difficult for women as business casual pervades, presenting all sorts of gray areas for women. When in doubt, overdress classically.

Have you ever noticed that the most confident, often senior-most executives rarely sit up straight at a table, copiously taking notes? There is generally a relaxed and confident air about them. The best are yet very engaged because, rather than planning their book report of the meeting, they are experiencing the meeting, actively listening and speaking in turn. Don't get me wrong: If your role is to provide the notes for the meeting, make it the best book report of all time. But if it's not, think about your presence each day you walk in the office, each time you enter a meeting, or even when you get on a WebEx or conference call. This is your brand—cultivate it.

Advocate...

. . . for yourself, but also for your female peers and those coming behind you. Advocacy is not for special treatment or affirmative action. Advocacy is for parity in opportunity, treatment, and respect (and also in compensation, but that's another book).

In 2013, I had the privilege of attending an inaugural women's leadership event put on by Willis in London. The impetus of the event was actually the retirement of our company's highest-ranking female executive. An incredibly impressive woman, this particular woman's legacy will be strong. However, in retrospect, she said she was underwhelmed by her own contribution to the advocacy of other women while she was scaling the proverbial Everest of the male insurance world. She wanted this event to engender that kind of future support.

Now, I imagine that she still did a lot for other women (if we know one thing about our own gender, we females expect an awful lot of ourselves), but simply her observation made me think—what had I done for my female peers and junior associates to help position them for success in an industry where solving for female executive achievement was still more of a complex calculus algorithm to a male's simple math? By this point, the epiphanies of lacking parity for women in the insurance industry seemed to be everywhere for me, and this point on advocacy was a mighty explosion in my mind. Really, I hadn't done that much. I had always been serious about the advancement and training of junior associates, but this was true whether they were female or male. I could do more to raise awareness and be an advocate for female colleagues so that hopefully when I retire, I can be proud of this legacy.

How can each of us advocate? Be a mentor or a sponsor. These words get thrown around a lot, and I am quite pleased if these occur organically rather than in contrived situations, such as a prescription from human resources that everyone selects a mentor from a big list of people within the company. To me, it simply means to provide support and guidance to the individual and to help elevate that person within the organization. Get their name out; recommend them for new projects and opportunities. Require respect on their behalf. Push back when you hear unfair categorizations of strong women for traits that otherwise would be applauded in men.

As a mentor or sponsor, be flexible and understanding. This goes not just for women but also for men. When I flew to London for the conference I mentioned, my son Aidan was two months old. It was important to me to go, so I grabbed my baby and my mom, and we all hopped on a plane. I juggled an infant trying to cope with an eight-hour time change and a breast pump with the wrong voltage attachment. On a scale of stressful and complicated, it was up there. That is just one of my many difficult "working mom" stories, and I am only one of countless women who can share such experiences. But men are parents, too, and at the end of the day, advocating for flexibility will help everyone and will keep more fabulously capable women in the workforce, on their way up that ladder.

Innovate...

...by thinking differently. After all, it is highly likely that your perspective is different and therefore your approach to solving a problem unique. Your inimitable perspective is an asset you can take to the bank.

I listened to a panel at a diversity summit. The summit was focused on women, but this particular panel included a male of a non-Caucasian ethnicity (which is no doubt another underrepresented group in insurance). He ran procurement for a large multinational and said something that resonated immensely with me. If five teams of lawyers (or reinsurance brokers, or consultants, or any team really) come to him with a pitch for services, the crux of their offering will be largely the same. But a team that includes diversity of personnel includes diversity of perspectives if for no other reason than from diversity of formative experiences. Diversity of perspectives when brainstorming how to solve deeply complex problems must yield a broader potential list of solutions. A team that maintains this diversity, and with it a respectful discourse on building the best solution, will be on a better course for innovation—a better course for a better solution. I believe this to be categorically true when teams balance expertise with gender (and other) diversity. Innovation's best examples in our society may seem to point to individuals—a brilliant person with a unique idea. A Steve Jobs or an Elon Musk receives endless glory. But innovation in reality is brought to life through teams that game plan, strategize, and problem solve. Diversity of perspective, experience, thought, and approach are natural partners to maximizing thought innovation. So, in my opinion, any company with a solely white, male board is kidding itself when it believes it has this complexity covered. This is actually where I believe that pure experience may be trumped by diversity of perspective. If the insurance industry sits back and lets the current cycle of executive and board hiring exist, change will continue to be elusive because executive (and board) opportunities are often filled directly through an internal network of those closest to the current executives who typically have substantial tenure. Frankly, there isn't much diversity in that pool. Maybe, in order for companies to better innovate, years of experience should be trumped by diversity of perspective. It is at least worth consideration.

Finally, My Least Favorite but of Critical Importance: Escalate...

... issues of discriminatory and biased practices. Don't just laugh off comments because "you can handle it." Be earnestly helpful in building awareness.

Sometimes comments or actions are overtly inappropriate. However, in my experience, most are largely unintended and the source of long-held social and societal biases. These types of biases pervade daily working life and create challenges in perpetuity unless and until addressed. Oddly, the former (overtly discriminatory practices) should be somewhat easier, if more uncomfortable, to deal with. These include actions and practices that are clearly wrong, such as sexual harassment. There is considerable training within corporations today to deal with sexual harassment, what qualifies, and how to escalate such an issue. As such, I will leave that to the side, as at least some semblance of tools (and laws) exist to combat its presence. Nevertheless, it is the unintentional and/or unwitting biases that can be trickier both to identify and to maneuver. How does one appropriately build awareness without creating an uncomfortable work environment? After all, in my own personal experience, these biases are held by some I would consider to be huge supporters of mine, men (and sometimes even women) who have sponsored me throughout my career, many who have daughters for whom they want to have parity in opportunities. These are not bad people—categorically, quite the opposite. In saying this, one must recognize that I, too, am not above reproach; all of us have biases that manifest in our daily lives. The best we can do is to be more aware and consciously consider them so as to deliberately combat them. Casting blame or categorizing someone as "sexist" or "misogynistic" for their biases is pejorative and counterproductive. How negative are these names and, moreover, how terrible does it feel to ever be labeled? Totally counterproductive, especially as the goal is to raise awareness and improve parity in our working environment.

Let me give a few personal examples. First, a dear mentor of mine more than once commented that I should be assigned to a particular account because the reinsurance buyer was female. I finally had to assert that this categorically was not why I should be selected. I should be on an account because I improve the team and I solve problems in a way that the client appreciates. Moreover, the view that women prefer to work with women simply because they are women is painfully flawed. I want to work with the best. I'm agnostic as to whether that is a man or a woman. On the flip side, wouldn't we be up in arms if they said only a man should work on a certain team because the client was a man?

Another example came when our company decided to open a new office and a position to run that office needed to be filled. This required relocation for anyone within the company. I was a prime candidate given a number of reasons (including a large client local to this city, which took me there frequently), but I was never asked if I would be interested. I felt that it was assumed I would not relocate because my husband also has a career and ties to our current location. When I finally pressed the topic, this was affirmed. Admittedly, the timing was difficult and I would not have, for personal reasons, made the move. However, I was disappointed not to be asked. It seemed somehow unfair that a male candidate whose wife did not work outside the home would be automatically considered for this type of relocation opportunity and I would not. Shouldn't I have had the opportunity to consider it?

This final example, which in order of occurrence was actually the first of these instances, was a true wake-up call to the inherent and unfair biases that I would face. Our industry is a small one, and we interact with competitors, clients, and prospects on a regular basis in the small markets in which we operate. Our industry is also one that remains based at least partially on trusted customer-adviser relationships and includes substantial travel and too many business dinners. In one such instance, I was traveling with a client (a 40-something male) in Bermuda for reinsurance program marketing. I was the junior associate (a 20-something female) on the account, and the lead broker (a 40-something male) was also traveling in our group. This was a fairly common occurrence for me, being generally younger and definitively less male than the typical group I interacted with. Despite my age, I worked very hard, had strong client rapport, and had proven my ability to add effective discourse to our client work and marketing sessions. The lead broker, being a good mentor, included me in the trip for these reasons. On this occasion, prior to heading to dinner, we ran into a senior colleague from another office within our company. As the lead broker stayed to chat with him, I accompanied the client to order a drink. The colleague proceeded to ask the senior broker why he bothered to bring me along on such a trip—effectively asking, what could someone like me possibly add to these discussions? Next, he insinuated it must have had something to do with the clients' appreciation of young females in his entourage. When the lead broker relayed this to me, I was shocked, frustrated, ashamed, and furious all at the same time. None of this could have been further from the truth, and how quickly some man could toss aside my hard work and value in such an off-handed, unfair, and ignorant comment. The unfortunate thing is, I have heard similar comments spoken at any given time regarding many other females in my industry. Maybe not precisely the same, but of the same ilk. All generally unfounded, and each time undermining of the woman's business acumen. I vehemently sound off to this type of chatter, but I doubt I hear even a fraction of it. As women, we must stand firm to counteract such comments. We also need our male counterparts to help put a stop to this kind of prattle. It is biased and demeaning and simply way too easy to laugh off or, worse yet, repeat. Be an advocate for yourself and, in these instances, for other women.

These "inadvertent" comments must be appropriately but mindfully escalated, to create awareness instead of tension. They need not be handled delicately so as to walk on proverbial eggshells but rather, because the goal is to change the face of the issue, with alacrity. Take the person aside and have a mature, respectful conversation about how the comments affected you. Sometimes I find it oddly effective to put it in the context of their own daughter, if they have one. Assume that they didn't even realize the effect the comment would have. Approach it as though you are actually trying to change future behavior, not assign blame. As you consider your approach, think of the next generation of women that comes behind you. We have the ability to guide practices so the next generation has a more equitable footing, and that is an admirable legacy.

It is our opportunity to continue to promote the goal of breaking the glass ceiling, to recognize that the work is not yet done! While it seemed daunting and disappointing at first to me, it is actually an exciting opportunity to be engaged and to catalyze change. This kind of change requires grassroots efforts from the majority. It needs a lot of soldiers (in really good shoes). We can take up the baton to demonstrate ability, elevate your individual brand, innovate through a unique approach, advocate for other women, and, finally, escalate issues that inhibit women's ability to operate at the top of our game. Because the top of women's game goes right through the roof—and the glass ceiling.

Chapter 3

Building Your Personal Brand

Kimberly George
Senior Vice President, Health Care Adviser
Sedgwick

O n a four-hour flight, what began as small talk with the gentle-man seated next to me became a life memory, an aha moment, and a point in time not to be forgotten. The conversation started as many in-flight chats do, with a brief exchange about the departure and arrival cities, and then moved on to the inevitable question, "What do you do?"

My seatmate was an international executive with expertise in sales, building teams, and leadership. The descriptions he shared of his job and career were noticeably connected to his love of family, passion for photography, vision for new ventures, and desire to travel. His confidence and demeanor were both impressive and engaging. I proudly shared my role at Sedgwick and our work to transform traditional managed care products into products with emphasis on care management and quality health care embedded in the claims process. I focused on recognition of Sedgwick's leaders, our position and growth in the market, my peers and their accomplishments, and our suite of products. I raved about our company culture, the leadership of our CEO, technology tools, level of client engagement, sales strategy, and approach to business. And, in explaining what I do, I proudly shared that I was a single mother, raising my two daughters since before they were school age, and that I returned to my small hometown to see family as often as possible.

We spent time discussing a growth company's culture and key attributes that made Sedgwick successful. He inquired about ways in which I personally contributed to that success. My response centered on the organization, our teams, my peers, and the outcomes of those efforts. Similar to a professor with his student, my new mentor patiently redirected me to answer his question, "In what ways do you personally contribute to the success of Sedgwick?" With a slightly different approach, I shared my connection with clients and being a lead subject matter expert for sales and client services. I expanded upon my operational background, evolving the company's practice group, leading strategy, and product development. As the student, I was keenly aware of missing the mark with my answer. After carefully listening to my response, and with purposeful intent, he asked, "What is your brand?" He explained, "I understand Sedgwick's brand; you have explained that very, very well." Perplexed, I hesitated to respond. "How does your brand help your company?" he asked.

Not unlike many women in business, I was told early in my career that individual accolades I might receive were not mine alone and must be positioned for the team. Any focus on personal accomplishments would be perceived as bragging, self-promoting, and intimidating to coworkers. Regardless of my male counterparts' use of the word *I,* for women, the use was viewed as abrasive and indicative of the woman lacking the skill set to be a team player and leader. Because "we" had always been a more natural approach to conversation for me than "I," reinforced by the managerial feedback, pluralistic terms became the norm. Even when referencing a personal opinion or individual contribution, I addressed the subject from a "we" perspective.

Rarely did I speak openly about an accomplishment I achieved or my personal goals; rather I focused on "we," always quick to deflect conversations regarding my personal contributions.

From a young age I was a believer in the phrase "feedback is a gift and what you do with it is your own." With that in mind, I took feedback from managers to heart, with the goal of improving my approach and delivery for the betterment of the company and my future. Depending on the year and manager at the time, development feedback varied from working on specific personality traits to higher-level career advancement and development opportunities. At times, my focus was on tone, word usage, and facial expressions; at other points, my focus was on building inclusive teams, executive communication style, and leadership attributes. Whether feedback was from a 360-degree performance review or traditional performance review, I sought input and guidance from internal mentors, external sponsors, and career coaches. These individuals provided constructive feedback and supported my personal growth. Seeking feedback is a risk, but one that cannot be undervalued when it comes to growing as an individual and becoming the best "you" that you can be.

At other points in my career, having a visionary-strategic leadership style led some managers to say I was out for personal gain rather than a company win. Mentors helped me understand the importance of giving people time to think through an idea and buy in or offer acceptance. In time, I gained a deeper appreciation for various leadership styles, across the spectrum of visionary, strategic, and operational attributes. I came to recognize that some leaders fit only one style and are limited in their ability to shift their approach to address a particular organizational need, move a specific project forward, or drive performance at the right time. This gave me the push to keep working on finding balance in my own leadership style. Admittedly, I often embraced the style necessary to meet my manager's expectations, rather than the style necessary to achieve success in my role and ensure success of the team.

When my seatmate asked how my brand helped my company, I was at a loss. I felt I was synonymous with my company's brand and that being brand aware and a brand champion was, in large part, driving my professional success and organizational opportunities. Little did

I know that understanding my personal brand and being authentic in acting on it would bring not only me greater success but also my company. As the flight landed, I was bound and determined to learn more about personal branding, although I still admit it brought an uncomfortable twinge. At the forefront of my angst was the realization that creating a personal brand would force me to become comfortable with the uncomfortable—acknowledging my personal contributions, along with my status as an industry thought leader; word choice, such as use of the word *I* rather than my comfort zone of pluralisms—and most definitely to become comfortable and confident in my leadership style, which would bring greater success to me and the company.

To my amazement, there were plenty of online resources and mentors to support creating a personal brand. I quickly engaged with both females and males who had boosted their careers and had doors open as a result of their brand. Creating a personal brand forces you to define your personal passions and align those with your career. Like leadership, branding is a personal journey. I encourage you to consider your personal brand as unique; no textbook or blog post has the answers to your brand and what will derive your personal happiness and business success. Wonderful advice I received early on in my branding development phase was to focus on consistency and not differentiation. Be true to yourself, be authentic, and your brand will be natural.

As I worked through personal attributes that are paramount to my brand, being a mother, daughter, and friend were not forgotten. My daughters have grown up in our single-parent household, and we live nearly 2,000 miles from my family. Regardless of how fiercely independent I might be, having loving, caring, and consistent help for my daughters was always critically important to me and never far from my thoughts. There was no place I would rather be than home, and while my daughters know that, they are also quick to acknowledge their desire to have a career that they love as much as I love mine. They are old enough to respect and appreciate what my career has afforded them and our family.

When my oldest daughter left for her first year of college earlier this month, inevitably I reflected on my own experience moving out of my parents' house 30 years ago. Imagine the shock my parents faced when at 17 years old, a few short weeks before my senior year of high school, I sprung on them that I hoped to enter college instead. Unbeknown to my parents, I planned to move hours from home, pay for college working as a certified nursing aide, and pursue a childhood dream of becoming a nurse. Their response was overwhelmingly supportive, regardless of their fears for my well-being, questions, and concerns. I am touched by their unconditional love and forever grateful that their unwavering support instilled a level of resilience and perseverance within me to overcome any challenge.

My work family means the world to me, and two of my Twitter hashtags, consistent with my personal brand, include #workisfun and #friendsarefamily. When you love what you do and the people you get to do it with, work and life are so much more meaningful. Being a working and frequently traveling single mom is not a typical attribute to choose as part of a personal brand. But for me, being true to my authentic self, being a mom, daughter, and friend must be part of my brand.

Branding is social, and where better to place emphasis on my brand than on social media? I strengthened my LinkedIn profile to reflect more of my personal brand. Then I actively and regularly began to engage with others on the site. I initially requested connections with people I knew or those in similar careers to mine and individuals with careers that interested me. I joined a few groups that aligned with my personal and corporate brands and soon began to see the results of my efforts. By creating an appealing personal brand, I saw my connections increasing dramatically. These were people primarily seeking me out for advice, networking, and thought leadership. Through networking with other health care experts, the vision evolved for forming the LinkedIn group "Transforming Healthcare for Tomorrow." This is a group in which the members are passionate about current news on health-related matters, and it has resulted in significant opportunities for my brand and that of my company.

My good friend and social media mentor, Jonathan Mast, Sedgwick's social media director, suggested I join Twitter. At the time Jonathan made the suggestion, a tweet was as foreign to me as personal branding was when my seatmate suggested it. He reminded me that, just like personal branding, social media must be consistent, authentic, and, by providing value, critically important to your connections. When I made the commitment to align my brand with social media, I knew straightaway there was a significant work effort. To be consistent on social media requires a high level of personal engagement. I am a voracious reader, and, historically, reading was strictly personal. Choosing to engage with social media and align it with my brand required training my mind to think differently. It meant identifying meaningful and relevant industry news to share in an engaging manner. Your network wants to experience more than your company's marketing or your own blog posts. I think the hardest part might be giving others a view into your life. Social media has significantly advanced my thought leadership position in health care, insurance, and workers' compensation with nearly 25,000 followers, each of whom enlightens me with knowledge I would never have had without this amazing community.

As mature leaders often share, real leadership opportunities came when they realized leadership is about service. For me, recognizing that I wanted to give back to the industry in which I have worked for more than 25 years was an important part of my brand. Today, I am a proud board member of Kids' Chance of America, a charity offering scholarships to children of employees catastrophically injured or killed while on the job. I am both grateful and humbled that my personal brand and outreach led to many organizations' becoming Kids' Chance partners and committing to give multiyear, six-figure donations to the charity. When a friend in the business asked me to join a small group of women and assist with creating a women's networking and leadership group, I jumped at the opportunity. Engaging women in leadership discussions, mentoring and career development, and bringing the broader industry together to address gender gap and diversity and inclusion was right up my alley and aligned perfectly with my company and personal brands. As a proud board member of the Alliance of Women in Workers' Compensation, I am actively engaged with creating and supporting their national and regional events, as well as spearheading the local ambassadors program across the country. Along with that line of service came the opportunity to fill a seat on the Workers Compensation Research Institute (WCRI) core funders committee. My thought leadership and operational claims and managed care background were a nice fit for the WCRI committee focused on medical and disability research. These are a few service examples of how I live my brand and how, through my engagement, my company benefits in a positive way.

For those who follow me, I consistently and with purpose address topics centering around leadership; business; health care; human resources and benefit programs; risk management and insurance; employee health, well-being, and productivity; health technology and digital health; population health and cultures of health; evolving health care delivery models; and patient engagement, experience, and safety. I regularly tweet, post, speak, and blog on the topics relevant to my brand. In a nutshell, or elevator speech as some like to reference, I am a chief health care strategist focusing on improving patient experience and health care delivery and transforming employee benefits. Listening and listening deeply, asking questions, and staying engaged with experts in the fields of insurance, health and health policy, health technology and innovation, human resources, and employee benefits and design experts, my company's position in the marketplace and organizational awareness has significantly increased. My company is engaged with conversations and routinely exposed to new opportunities that are directly tied to my brand.

As my personal brand grew, so did requests for me to speak at conferences, attend industry thought leadership events, and respond to media inquiries. My company does a great job at managing my engagement to ensure events and requests align with the company's brand or my personal brand. A few years ago, Sedgwick's marketing and communications department decided to align me with another thought leader in the industry: Mark Walls of Safety National. Mark has amassed more than 25,000 followers in his Work Comp Analysis Group. Given that each of us has a personal brand with a large following, our companies created Out Front Ideas with Kimberly and Mark. The OFI educational series focuses on topics in the workers' compensation and health care industry that are not given enough attention in mainstream media or conference outlets. The show is brought to our audience by way of webinars and live conference sessions. It has proven to draw more participants than the largest conference keynote addresses. I am fortunate to work with a team that maximizes my brand for the greater good of the company.

For me, building a brand was very personal. Other than a few trusted mentors and inquiries about branding, I embarked on creating a personal brand alone, without my company's direction or a coach's guidance. I am forever grateful for my seatmate's advice on that flight nearly seven years ago. I trusted that branding would be good for my career and my company, and it was a win-win that my company embraced my brand with as much passion as I embrace the company's brand.

Within two years of launching my personal brand, a CEO in the pharmacy benefits space suggested my company nominate me for the *Business Insurance* Women to Watch. My company had a great history and track record of nominating clients for industry awards; however, we had not yet nominated one of our own to be recognized by the industry. I am fortunate that Sedgwick's president and CEO, Dave North, not only understood the value to my brand in being named a Woman to Watch, but also recognized the company's brand exposure and value in becoming an active sponsor and participant in the Women to Watch conference over the past five years. Being recognized as a Woman to Watch in 2011 was monumental for me. The angst I faced in those early months of creating a personal brand and becoming comfortable with the uncomfortable was all worth it.

At Sedgwick, our subject matter experts, including me, work with our marketing and senior management using an annual thought leadership approach to bring forward the topics and perspectives that are most important to our audiences. Our collective goal is to be on the forefront of what is or could be most important to drive the conversation and service delivery in our industry forward. For me, that means speaking at conferences, hosting webinars, blogging, and promoting across social media on a variety of health care–related topics, as well as addressing the political, technological, and legislative landscape surrounding reform. Because of my interest and expertise in these areas, my company was able to promote my messages through Sedgwick-organized activities and mass-marketing platforms. And in turn, I use my personal brand to promote the company's message platform. It is this symbiotic relationship and respect of both company and personal brand marketing that has made Sedgwick an ideal place for me to grow my career.

By sharing my experiences and through my thought leadership activities, I am hopeful the next generation of women in the workplace will have greater confidence and opportunities to overcome diversity and inclusion challenges. Use of the word *I* is not harmful to your career, and the most successful executives understand that individual contribution is important for team success. Seeking feedback from others is a personal growth tool that I highly recommend. However, feedback should not put you in an "analysis paralysis" state or make you constantly question your abilities. Take a thoughtful approach to assess the feedback and identify the points that will improve your skill sets and ultimately bring personal and professional success. And, finally, be true to your leadership style. We cannot mirror ourselves with each manager; rather, own your own style and, with that, grow to be a well-rounded peer, mentor, and team member with appreciation for all leadership styles.

Seven years ago, I boarded a flight and never expected my seatmate, Tom Dendy, and our conversation would be life changing. Tom has an incredible career reputation as an international business leader, mentor and coach, speaker, and venture investor. His business connections are worldwide and cross industry sectors from manufacturing to health care. Tom is quick to share a story about his family, wife Shelley, and sons Tim and Tyler. Family is as much a part of Tom's brand as it is mine. I now look for "seatmate moments"—times when I can offer positive influence to others, whether it is in an individual conversation or more formal mentoring and coaching. Give back to others and invest in their careers. You never know how important it will be to them, and I promise you, you will get more out of it than you can ever imagine. Thank you, Tom, for all you have done to support my personal and career growth and for openly sharing your wisdom.

Chapter 4

Hear Me Roar

Caryn Siebert
Vice President and Chief Claims Officer
Knight Insurance Group

G rowing up in New York as a kid, most of my female role models were elementary school teachers—yes, even my mom! Lawyers, doctors, politicians, local business owners, sports figures, and stockbrokers who surrounded me personally or via my parents were all men. So when I told my parents I wanted to be a veterinarian or a lawyer, it was clear I was going to break the pattern set by friends and relatives.

Fast-forward—not only did I get into law school, but I graduated at the top of my class. One of the largest law firms in the country hired me, and I found some female role models at the firm and at the carriers/brokers with whom I interacted. They and others after them in Chicago, Kansas, Seattle, and California have been influencers in shaping my career. Now I take pride in being a mentor and coach to several female professionals as well as high school and college girls. Naturally, I also mentor and coach male colleagues as we groom them for future roles as well.

Mentoring

Having been on the 2010 Women to Watch list, the president of a national third-party administrator, and now the chief claims officer at a major carrier within a $6 billion holding company, mentorship is key. My career has included several terrific experiences and moves across the country with memorable mentors. Mentors can teach you a variety of things ranging from how to select wine, organize events for 12 people or 1,200 people, and think creatively. I was with one of my mentors and we needed to check into our hotel rooms. His room was ready, but the hotel was oversold so there was no room for me. He looked at the hotel clerk and calmly asked her a simple question. He said, "If President Reagan showed up tonight, would you have a room for him?" She smiled and said, "But of course; he's the president of the United States," to which he replied, "Well, President Reagan isn't coming, so Ms. Siebert will take his room." That was such a polite, calm, and creative way to obtain a room for me—though admittedly he took that presidential suite and I took his original room, but it was so memorable. I learned a lot from him in that one evening, and 20 years later I still share the story. Thanks, Courtney!

But my favorite mentoring moments relate to being able to coach team members, be they colleagues, peers, or direct reports, as to what I call managerial courage. As a leader who exhibits managerial courage, I am known as a leader who "tactfully dispenses direct and actionable feedback; is open and direct with others without being intimidating; and deals head-on with people, problems, and prickly situations." By the way, I should probably insert the word *usually* because even I get stressed and am human. Just the other day I felt compelled to apologize to my team for having a "Snickers" commercial moment, as I just wasn't myself. However, it even takes courage to admit to your team when you aren't at your best.

If there is one quality that distinguishes great leaders, respected team managers, or even high-potential employees, in my opinion it is managerial courage. And you don't need to be a manager of people to have managerial courage. More often than not, uncertainty, the need to make decisions rapidly, unclear lines of responsibility, and contradictory demands from different stakeholders all necessitate managerial courage. Courage must also be expressed every day, at every level in the business world. In the world of insurance claims, for example, it takes quite a bit of managerial courage for a claims service representative to advise a claimant that their policy doesn't cover their date of loss, or for a claims resolution examiner to explain to a claimant that the policy limit has already been exhausted, or that their truck wasn't listed on the schedule of vehicles, or that they missed the statute of limitations. Defusing those situations takes tremendous courage.

My company expects its employees to act with courage in many circumstances, yet we don't expect employees to take willy-nilly risks. The authors of *The Courage to Act* highlighted various domains in which courage is critical to performance. This is my twist on their thoughts.

- **Courage to face the truth and to express it to others**

Many people prefer not to admit there is a problem, rather than recognize it and be forced to respond. The lack of courage is therefore often insidious because it is easier for people to think of themselves as cowards or not empowered. Furthermore, being aware of a problem is not sufficient if one does not dare to express it out loud. At every company, there are impassioned hallway discussions/water-cooler chats where people vigorously express what they would have liked to say in a meeting "if they could have."

- **Courage to rely on others**

A second form of courage indispensable to companies is daring to rely on others. Everyone knows that efficient delegation is critical to performance. However, the degree of courage to delegate is generally underestimated: you must be ready to relinquish control over results and share information. In reality, information when shared is even more powerful. Working effectively in teams requires this form of courage. There are particular team members who at times are so hesitant to relinquish control that they end up falling behind and negatively impacting the team. At the same time, these people are some of the best in terms of empowering their teams with other issues and being great teachers. Several of them are going to be fabulous leaders once they attain the right balance regarding relying on others.

One of my leadership models is Wayne Gretzky, known in hockey as "the great one," and yet he was all about the team. He would keep the other 11 players on the ice all in his sight, anticipate what others would do, pass the puck to teammates to take shots, learn from mistakes, and celebrate victories together while always giving back to the community.

- **Courage to make decisions in risky or uncertain situations**

Making decisions without being able to weigh the consequences in detail or to collect all desired information is difficult but essential. Companies need employees who are able to show initiative, which may sometimes mean daring to take action without receiving prior approval from superiors, for example. Conversely, someone can be courageous in deliberately choosing not to take action despite pressure from stakeholders. My current company is very focused on enterprise risk management and that entails facing risks head on and exercising managerial courage. By expecting the unexpected, one avoids being shocked.

- **Courage to work outside our comfort zone**

Top-performing teams are those that dare to move outside the comfort of what they know and push the limits. Setting ambitious objectives and having the persistence to pursue them in the face of adversity is a particularly critical form of courage in the business world. When confronted with a situation that is relatively satisfying, who is willing to be the disruptor and attempt to take something from good to great? I received a thank you note in April 2015 from a female colleague. The note read: "I appreciate you always pushing me to the limits and working outside of my comfort zone. You enabled me to be a better employee as a result, and I appreciate the chances you took on my development."

- **Courage to impose rigorous standards**

Finally, a dimension that is often underestimated consists of imposing discipline and rigor on others and ourselves. I pride myself on finding the "diamonds in the rough" and drawing the best out of them on a regular basis. Now, I also am a believer in Marcus Buckingham's Strength Finder and possess "maximize" as a signature theme, so being aware of that strength is key as it can just as easily become a weakness.

It takes a lot of motivation to define obligations whose benefits may not be visible in the short term. As a leader I sometimes struggle with the marathon versus sprint concept. But as a believer in managerial courage, I also say, "don't let perfection be the enemy of better!" (Thanks, Chan.) And I work relentlessly to ensure that these rules are applied, especially since others are unlikely to give thanks in return!

Speaking of thanks, I was recently given an amazing "gift" if you will. The first 90 days of joining a new team are critical. We join new teams all the time, whether we recognize it or not—new teams at work, new teams in sports, new teams in the family, and so on. Well, I recently joined Knight Insurance Group/Hankey Group, and thus joined three new teams all at once.

- I joined the Knight Executive Leadership Team as a team member reporting to the CEO of Knight with a half-dozen new peers;
- I joined the Knight Claims Leadership Team as the chief claims officer and leader of that team; and
- I joined the Hankey Group as one of 2,300 employee-owners founded by Don Hankey, a multibillionaire with whom I have daily conversations about business and life.

From January through June 2016, I met hundreds of people in my new role, displaying approachability, positivity, and energy, and utilizing managerial courage along the way. In July, my newfound colleagues presented me with a book full of handwritten notes. Certainly, a note from the CEO saying, "I have learned a lot from you and thank you," was cool, but I must say that the ones that were as impactful, if not more so, came from folks I had already been able to mentor. Let me share some examples, as it is my hope that the tidbits in this chapter will be my way of paying it forward such that you, too, can receive notes like this someday. It is also a way for me to pay an open homage to those who wrote these types of notes! They motivate me and are leaders in their own ways.

- "I am extremely proud to be led by a strong, smart, funny, and courageous woman like yourself and growing under your leadership."
- "Thanks for your energy, focus, and direct influence in your claims department and other departments throughout the company."

- "Thank you for letting our work colleagues know/feel how everything they do is important to the growth and well-being of our company."
- "You are a very caring and humble woman and we are lucky to have you as part of the Knight family, guiding us with patience and understanding."
- "You are truly the empowerment of our motto 'At Knight, we CARE,' and I look forward to continuing to learn and grow under your mentorship."

Offering a final thought on mentorship, there are times when the best way to be a mentor is to just be there when a team member falls down and you help pick them up, lift them up, or otherwise encourage them. Personally, I am still learning and developing as a leader and mentor. Having been a president and CEO, it enables me to assist the presidents and CEOs with whom and for whom I now work in a different way with a deeper appreciation for the challenges they encounter. Yet I learn from them continually.

Succession Planning

Succession planning at all levels, and especially at the executive level and in the boardroom, should include consideration of high-potential women and the investments to be made in their development. Assisting through payment of coaching, organizational memberships, or participation in groups focused on development is helpful. It also helps facilitate women meeting other female role models. I look back over the years and have helped be a positive influence on many who have advanced. With the advent of Facebook and LinkedIn, I'm constantly amazed by how many of us keep in touch and share stories about kids, partners, parents, or careers. They sit on boards, run their own companies, are business executives, help the PTA, participate on not-for-profit boards, and/or are troop leaders. They are amazing and lead multidimensional lives.

While I was president of a third-party administrator, over 50 percent of our workforce and extended leadership team was female, including our chief financial officer, controller, and various service leaders/account managers. Until I brought in another woman, I was the only female member of the board of directors. Yet, thanks to my parents and loving baseball, horse racing, football, and the stock market, I have always been able to hold my own in conversations with male colleagues. All of that comes into play when it comes to succession planning and interacting with colleagues in determining their talent.

Succession planning is a process for identifying and developing internal people with the potential to fill key business leadership positions in the company. Succession planning increases the availability of experienced and capable employees who are prepared to assume these roles as they become available. Thus, succession planning in my mind means interacting with employees outside of just the four walls of work. Succession planning is a philosophy, a company practice, and not an isolated project. As such, it must be practiced consistently, and I always have open discussions with my team members. "Hey, if I get hit by a bus, you all need to know what has to be done." Or sometimes we'd kid around, especially my friend and colleague TB, who played the lottery like clockwork and said, "Hey, if a few of us hit the lottery together, who would jump in and take over our roles?" Internal candidates should be developed and in some cases realigned to allow the growth of others capable of ascending to various assistant vice president, vice president, and higher levels.

Some companies expect the unexpected. *Successful* companies plan for the unexpected. And I always say that if you expect the unexpected, you'll not be caught off-guard. The best talent in an organization is cultivated over time and understands the culture of the company as much as, if not more than, the technical information. Time and time again, I am invited to be a speaker at industry events. In recent years, it's been my pleasure to not only say yes but to also have a colleague as a co-presenter to develop them and broaden the team's talent. Brandon, Robin, Mark, Bert, Monica, John, Samantha, and others moved from being surprised about selection to looking forward to being presenters in their own right. We all are fortunate when we get to the point of being successful through others and allowing them to shine. It also inspires other peers and colleagues, while allowing the organization's image to flourish through multiple demographics. Who are those talented individuals on your bench?

I am blessed to work for a company where the founder (thank you, Don) has created an employee stock ownership plan (ESOP) so that everyone—women obviously included—can have an ownership interest in the company. Half of my claims leadership team is female, and I coach and mentor men and women across multiple generations and profiles. They know my expression about moving ahead as ducks (yes, even in a VUCA world, Eric)—paddling like crazy under the surface but gliding smoothly atop the water at eye level. We work hard, have fun, and swim together toward our goals while appreciating one another's differences as much as similarities. Also like ducks, when we fly we do so in such a way to know our roles and fly in a "V," so to speak. By doing so, at different parts of the journey each of us takes the lead, which helps us to conserve energy. Excluding the individual leading the group, each of us as ducks trailing behind the other benefits from a reduction in wind resistance so we all make it further. Thus, we are always in succession mode and learning how to be one another's backups.

How many of you reading this right now can remember the last time you took a two-week vacation while you were holding down a full-time job? I pose this question because if you haven't, it is my opinion that you are doing yourself and your team a disservice. You are missing a terrific opportunity to concomitantly recharge, mentor, and succession plan. The first two to three days of vacation you are worried about what you are leaving behind and neglecting. The last two to three days of vacation you are worried about what you are coming back to and how issues were handled. So when were you actually disconnected and vacationing if you only took off a week? Taking off that extra week truly allows you to decompress (yes, mom, I glance at e-mail while on vacation, but for me that's still decompressing), but it also enables your team to lead. To demonstrate to you that they are quite capable of running things in your absence, learning what they can't do, and perhaps even truly appreciate what you make look so easy.

Taking some excerpts from the same thank you booklet that I referenced earlier, these are some other quotes that I feel relate to succession planning.

- "I am forever grateful for you helping us to see the greatness within ourselves where we learn, dream, and do more."

- "I am thankful for the trust you have shown in my capabilities and grateful for your mentorship, kindness, thoughtfulness, and inspiration."
- "Thanks for being a great role model, not only as a leader but for all of us women fighting and working for better pay and opportunities."

Each of these comments relate to bringing the best out of employees and letting them rise to the occasion. What a great way to find and groom future leaders of people, process, and product. Golda Meir once said, "Trust yourself. Create the kind of self that you will be happy with all your life. Make the most of yourself by fanning the tiny, inner sparks of possibility into flames of achievement." As a leader and mentor, especially in considering succession planning, you must spark others, too!

Coming full circle to my earlier comments as to marathon versus sprint, since my years at General Electric, I have stuck to a simple succession planning four-quadrant philosophy:

- Ready now,
- 12 to 18 months,
- 18 to 24 months, and
- Not likely to advance (due to either performance or potential).

Now, certainly, employees can shift from one quadrant to another over time, but it is critical to do a periodic review as to their skills, knowledge, and ability as well as their desire to pursue a leadership or a technical track. Within the leadership track, my advice would be to keep in mind that there are terrific leaders of people separate and apart from terrific leaders of process/product. The two do not always meet, and yet both are critical. Be their spark!

The topics of mentoring and succession planning also relate to encouraging those in the next generation. While I personally do not have any children, I am a godmother and have been a guide or mentor to the children of several friends inside and outside of the business. As an example, I met Ashley, the daughter of a coworker at my prior company, at a golf tournament we were sponsoring. I asked what she wanted to be when she grew up, and she uttered, "Miss California." Over the course of time, it was my pleasure to introduce Ashley to

Miss Orange Show; Miss Placentia; to Kids Konnected, which became her volunteerism platform; and to others. Her mom and she were very focused on making that dream come true, and I wanted to do my part in assisting. Well, she became Miss Teen Placentia, and while she did not advance to the next levels, we utilized her attaining the status of Miss Teen Placentia and Miss Congeniality at the overall competition in her college and related scholarship applications, as well as my letter of recommendation—and yes, she starts Berkeley in the fall of 2016. This new generation—call them Millennials, call them Generation Z, it doesn't matter—has dreams and aspirations, and we can assist them in avoiding pitfalls and make those dreams a reality.

Take the time to write those letters of recommendation, to open doors, to assist them in receiving scholarships, and to encourage them to interview for roles, even if only to get interview experience and to meet amazing people. Julianna from Florida wanted an internship in New York, and I was proud to share my virtual Rolodex with her and support that goal. It's a blessing to be able to pay it forward and so cool to receive LinkedIn invitations from Brian, Chris, Samantha, Andrew, Matt, Joey, Julia, Jonathon, Austin, Nicholas, and others, who are now young adults and take to heart things we talked about at pool parties or drum line when they were kids.

Speaking of scholarships, along with a great committee and a fabulous leader named John, as chair of the Combined Claims Conference (CCC), it's been a wonderful experience creating an educational scholarship program for CCC. Too often, companies cut training from their budgets. So another way I can train those new to the industry and create a stronger bench is through our committee giving out over 300 scholarships which we distribute annually. PEO is a terrific ladies group that also gives out scholarships to young women. The Insurance Professionals of Orange County, various divisions of the Risk and Insurance Management Society (RIMS), National Retail & Restaurant Association (NRRDA), and the National Association of Insurance Women are all great examples of groups encouraging the next generation of insurance professionals to develop in the industry. The Claims Litigation Management Alliance (CLM), with Adam Potter at the helm as an entrepreneurial leader, is another fabulous training resource for various aspects of the insurance industry. As prior winners of the

Women to Watch, how are you paying it forward through these and other groups to fund the future? Let's share those opportunities and keep up the momentum.

Moving Forward and Final Thoughts

There was a 1970s song, "I Am Woman" by Helen Reddy, that says, "I am woman, hear me roar, in numbers too big to ignore, and I know too much to go back an' pretend … no one's ever gonna keep me down again." Now we are in 2016, and Helen Reddy would be so proud. Whether you like them or not (that's a different issue), think about Oprah Winfrey, Condoleezza Rice, Anne Fudge, Meg Whitman, Hillary Clinton, Janet Yellen, Ruth Ginsberg, Arianna Huffington, Suze Orman, Mary Barra, and I could go on. How far we have come.

I am so proud to be on the *Business Insurance* Women to Watch list, to have been an Ernst & Young Entrepreneur of the Year Finalist, and to be a daily positive influence on female colleagues in the insurance, risk, and legal community.

There's a new book coming out titled *Out Front* by a friend of mine, Deborah Shames, who is the founder of Eloqui. Deborah commented to a large group recently that she believes women "strive for perfection out of fear." That women want to do well, want to be a good girl, are afraid someone will ask a question they can't answer or just want to make others proud. When it comes to speaking, Deb says she sees women "over-prepare, write things out, memorialize, and read their presentations and lose their audience." She also comments that roughly 80 percent of the import of any message is delivered nonverbally, so how do you roar in a nonverbal fashion?

As I wrap up this chapter, it is my pleasure to share something from two dear friends. Scott Grossberg provided me with his book entitled *The Most Magical Secret,* and in tribute to you, Scott, I say for myself, and I encourage others to stop and say:

- I can.
- I will.
- I dare.
- I am.

- I can accomplish the impossible.
- I dare to be passionately curious.
- I do whatever it takes.
- Take my heart and set it on fire such that I may give it to the world.
- I am Magic.
- We all have brilliance within; let it shine through.

My good friend Kimberly Roush shared her book titled *When I am BIG*. As a thank you to Kimberly, I share the following:

When I am big, **I am a social butterfly: I am**
Outgoing and social with others
Engaging and enthusiastic
Smiling and humorous
Being generous in giving my time, money and assistance

When I am big, **my ideas and actions are big: I am**
Creative and innovative
Trustworthy and a great confidante
Motivated to bring my "A" game to the table personally and
professionally
Getting others involved and rallied
Encouraging others
Trusting my gut and expressing my opinions
Working with teams to tackle seemingly insurmountable challenges

When I am big, **I help others be big: I am**
Taking time to mentor people and bring out their best
Willing to take on more without being asked
Showing my gratitude
Offering positive insights
Accessing, strategizing and collaborating so we all reach great results
Learning and trying new concepts together

When I am big, **my personal life is big: I am**
Travelling to new places
Being an understanding and loving daughter
Feeling empowered to move full speed ahead
Taking time to exercise, be at a sporting event or read
Doing things for others though I may not receive anything in return
I am BIG and help others be BIG!

The sharing of those two items is a way for me to pay it forward to those of you who are reading this chapter. As you mentor and lead others, don't forget about yourself. What are you like when you are at your personal and professional best? How do you maintain the balance? When you get up each day and interact with others, how do you leave them feeling after that special encounter? Will they seek out your opinion, assistance, and participation again?

So to my fellow Women to Watch, hear me roar and let's continue to be role models at work, at home, and in life, especially to those still on the rise!

Chapter 5

Lessons Learned in a 30-Year Career

Carol Arendall
Vice President Safety & Risk Management
US Foods, Inc.

C ollege was a long time ago, and when I think back to "how smart I was back then," I realize how lucky I was to find a fulfilling career in an area I never even knew existed when I graduated. I, like many, stumbled into the risk management field early on and grew to love the pace and variety of the role. As I reflect back on my 30-plus years, it's clear that our world is a relatively small world of professionals. People have long-term memories when it comes to others' mistakes. Good behavior and professionalism are important at all points in your journey. Strange as it sounds, I can still recall the people who made fools of themselves at company events or conferences 15 years ago. You do not want to carry that baggage with you for the rest of your career, so behave!

Align yourself with people who are smarter than you. You cannot be the smartest person in the room all the time. Trust those people and their opinions. It's okay to change your mind when you receive input from experts. Changing your mind does not make you look weak. Instead, it shows you are open and willing to grow and learn. Collaboration is truly the key to success. You will get buy-in from your colleagues when you take a little of their view and opinion and craft it into your final solution. Everyone wants to be part of the solution.

Relationships matter. People you meet early on in your career can come back into your world later on in your career, so you want to be sure that you maintain an impeccable reputation. Sometimes that's all we have when we are meeting with colleagues. Be the professional who is honest and trustworthy and not trying to take the last nickel off the table. Business deals are an equation in which both parts need to feel at least equal or perhaps slightly ahead. If your goal is to always win on the deal, you will run out of people to sit across the table with you. Be sensitive to what matters in a negotiation. Sometimes you may have to compromise on something you really want, but if it gets you closer to the ultimate goal of closing the deal, then be ready for it.

If you are really fortunate, as I have been, you will align yourself early in your career with people who become your lifelong colleagues. I have relationships that extend throughout my entire career—people I can trust and who I know are working in my best interest. As I have changed jobs and roles, these are the people I count on to help me master the challenges. My lifelong colleague Elsa Lynch was my insurance broker and client executive at Marsh. We met when we were in our 20s, young mothers trying to navigate our jobs, our companies, and our industries. We learned a lot in those early years, both the technical aspects of our positions as well as the hard lessons of balancing work life and home life. I am not sure we always got it right, but I do know the journey was wonderful. I often tell colleagues to "find their Elsa," that one person who has your back.

Never stop learning. The world is ever changing with new products and services. Do not be afraid to try new things. I remember back in 1987 when the excess liability market tightened and Marsh came to me proposing a new risk transfer vehicle called Ace, which had a unique hybrid claims-made policy. We bought into the Ace concept, which at the time required you to purchase Ace stock in an amount equal to your premium. Never at that time did I expect that Ace would become the dynamic insurance market leader that they became.

Embrace technology and be willing to change past practices, but do not lose sight of personal connections. I was around long before the Internet and e-mail and look back on how much has changed by adding those two technical innovations. The whole world sped up around me, and expectations grew around immediacy. E-mail and text are great, but do not hesitate to pick up the phone or meet with colleagues face to face. Sometimes it is important to look at someone across the table to get an understanding of what is needed.

Do not be afraid of a career change. I spent almost 20 years in one job and made a job move where I stayed for five years and then made another job change. We are never too old for change. It is energizing, and you would be surprised how much your experience in other industries and roles can be relevant in your new role.

Be sensitive to your colleagues' life outside of work. Flexible job arrangements are optimal for people with a number of outside commitments. It may not necessarily be due to children and child care issues. Many employees are challenged with aging parents. Some employees just want the opportunity to flex their creative muscles in another area entirely, such as music or writing. I was blessed to have a flexible job early in my career when there were not many employers interested in it. What it did was build a tremendous amount of loyalty in me for my company. Many employees are willing to trade salary for flexibility.

Encourage your employees to use all of their vacation time and when they are on vacation—be on vacation. Everyone deserves time away from work. Set the right expectation for your employees. If you absolutely must talk to your employees while they are on vacation, limit the time and scope.

Set realistic expectations on working hours and tell prospective employees how many hours outside of the office you expect from them. If you want employees to stop checking their phones at 7 P.M. outside of work, then stop e-mailing and texting them after 7 P.M.

Be a mentor. There are many young people coming up through our industry; take the time to help develop them. We owe it to our employers as well as our industry to groom the next generation of risk professionals.

Lead them by example as well as by taking time to coach and counsel. Do not tell the next generation what to do but rather be there as a guidepost. No one learns when someone else tells them what to do.

Perhaps one of the most important lessons I learned later on in my career is to embrace diversity. People tend to gravitate to people who look like they do or think like they do. It keeps your lens of the world very narrow. In my current role at US Foods, I work in a department that has joined a number of people from different backgrounds and cultures to create a mix of thought and talent. It is incredibly refreshing to work with a group that has a completely different view of the world than I do.

Be an advocate for diversity at your workplace in both employees and vendors. Look closely when a firm says they are minority-owned. Be sure it is not just window dressing. True diversity should be natural and not forced. If you are scavenging the landscape looking for diverse firms or job candidates, then perhaps you are looking in the wrong places. There are plenty of diversity network groups that can point you in the right direction.

Be happy and have some fun at work. It is perfectly okay to laugh a little. Set the tone for others. If you are grumpy, you can be sure others around you will take on some of your tone. Even when you are not always feeling it, try to put on a positive persona. If you are a leader, you will be surprised how much your positive tone will rub off on colleagues. People gravitate toward positive colleagues. I have enjoyed many Friday mornings in the office leading the early arrivers in some line dancing. Yes, line dancing. Why? Because it is fun and people in my office look to me bring on the fun. For the record, I am an awful dancer, so I believe deep down it makes others feel way more accomplished than the VP of Safety & Risk Management! This may not work for everyone, but it works for me. If ever there are meetings or events requiring some unashamed dancing, you can count on me.

Anyone who has had a career as long as I have at some point mishandles a situation or problem. How you recover from it is the key. Early on in my career I had a budget meeting with my chief financial officer (CFO) and he was raking me over the coals asking me to defend my budget. I had that epic moment when I lost my concentration and I had tears sprinkle down from my eyes. Oh, the horror!

I won't actually say the CFO was amused, but he was not exactly upset that he got a few tears out of me. I pushed through the rest of the meeting and made a vow that would never happen to me again. Going forward, for every budget meeting after that, I was completely prepared for every question and pushback he gave me. I even made copies of checks of money that I brought in the door on subrogation recoveries. No CFO can argue with money in the door.

Be clever and think outside of your own job and try to make your surroundings better. As a result of my habit of showing off recovery checks to my CFO, I asked him if I recovered an extra $100,000 on subrogation matters whether I could use that money to remodel the women's restroom on my floor at the office, which was in desperate need of updating. It was 30 years old if it was a day. Sure enough, with a goal of remodeling the women's restroom, I was able to recover $120,000, and I got permission to remodel the men's and women's restrooms. I was a hero to my coworkers, who, on the day of the bathroom reopening, had a pizza party and a plaque dedicated to me, which hung above the door to the women's restroom until the day I left the company. Today, the "Carol Arendall Memorial Bathroom" plaque sits humbly on my wall in my basement. Strange as it may sound, it was one of my biggest accomplishments because it was totally outside my core job and it just made peoples' lives better.

There will always be difficult people in the workplace. How you deal with them can truly set you apart as a leader. It is never going to work to exacerbate the situation and be difficult in return to another difficult person. We have a saying here at my employer, US Foods, "Keep it above the line." In other words, do not disparage a colleague no matter how difficult they are to deal with. Try to find some common ground, if possible. Focus on the problem solving, not the problem storytelling. I have generally found that the less comfortable someone is in their job, the more likely they will be difficult to work with. If you add bluster to your words, perhaps no one will notice that you are weak in your role. Eventually, people will figure it out. If you have a difficult coworker, you need to try even harder to make it work.

What if you hate—truly hate—your job? Leave. No amount of money is ever worth staying at a job you truly hate. Do not just quit in a fit of rage, but start looking. Sometimes just looking for another job and seeing that your skills are valued by other employers will help make you feel better. However, you should still leave. Be diligent and find the next right opportunity.

How do you know when you select the right new job? Listen to your gut. Much as we try to go against our gut sometimes and go for the big money, it may not make you happy. Sure, the extra money makes life a little easier, but if you are expected to work 80 hours a week, you should take a pause and think about it. Will that type of job commitment work for you at this point in your life?

What if you need to relocate for a new position? This works for some and not for others. We all have different commitments. There is no universal right answer. I have had a few opportunities to relocate for some really big jobs, but I chose to stay close to home. Now more than ever, I am glad I did as I deal with an aging parent who lives minutes from me. Aging parents are challenging but even more so when you are not geographically close.

All of this advice gets us to the heart of the matter. Be a leader in your organization. You should be more than just your job title. Leadership is cross-functional. Be the leader people want to follow, not the leader who demands. As a leader, you are only as good as your team. Keep developing the talent below you instead of looking for opportunities to manage up. If your team is strong and you keep achieving your overall goals, recognition will come.

Keep in mind that every member of your work team is important, and it is just as important to manage down as it is to manage up. We all know to put our best suit on when we are meeting with the CEO and to practice multiple times what you are going to say when you get that magical moment with your CEO. The problem for most of us is that the number of meetings with the CEO will be limited. How do you prepare when you meet with your full team? Every person on that team is important, so value all of them. Be sure to have an agenda that shows some thought and foresight before you meet. Let team members know what is expected of them when you meet. They should also be prepared.

How do you know if you are a leader or a manager? Three hundred sixty–degree interviews are quite good at getting feedback. If your organization does not believe in this type of spend for these interviews, perhaps your human resources department has someone who can assist you with this. As important as it is for you to believe you are successful, it is critical that you know what others think of you. One of our cultural values at US Foods is called "Straight Talk." It sounds catchy, but in reality it is not an easy thing to deliver. We all like delivering good news, but it is not easy to provide growth advice. My boss recently solicited feedback from me, and her exact words were: "I am not going to grow if you do not give me constructive feedback." That really is the way to think about it. We all want to be the best at our jobs, but if no one tells you how to be better, you will remain where you are.

Upon reflection of a long career, what would I have changed? I am sure there are many things I could have done better. I don't want to sound clichéd, but I really did sweat the small stuff. I should not have, since the small stuff was not going to make that much of a difference.

I have many people to thank for helping me be successful. I learned the basics from a risk management legend, Dave Haight, who was an early leader in the Risk and Insurance Management Society (RIMS). I then went on to work for Ann Roberts (at the time the director of risk management at Carson Pirie Scott) in my first real managerial position. Ann taught me so much, from where to sit in a meeting to when to be firm with a vendor and how to laugh at the chaos. Many of the fundamentals I learned from Ann remain with me today.

I am grateful for all the wonderful coworkers, vendors, and partners that I have crossed paths with throughout my journey. They are too numerous to name them all, but many I have cherished for 20 years or more.

As I close in on the sunset of my career, what am I the most proud of? Easy question. My family and being able to balance my career with a full home life. Sometimes when I am reading through the Sunday newspaper, I will flip through the obituaries. Creepy, I know, but I do it. Obituaries are a short paragraph meant to summarize a person's whole life in 200 words or less. I have never seen in an obituary "worked 80 hours a week," "never took a vacation," or "died peacefully with his cell phone in hand." If these three phrases sum up your work–life balance, please take notice. No one is going to care about this in the end. What will matter is the relationships you have created and those you love and those who love you. Never lose sight of that.

Chapter 6

The Myth of Work-Life Balance

Carolina Klint
President, U.S. South Zone
American International Group Inc.

I am a very lucky woman. I was born in a civilized country in a modern time. If you stop for a moment and think about it, such basics are actually still fundamental for a woman's opportunity to receive higher education, marry for love, and rule her own destiny. It is important to remember how lucky we are, and that sometimes it is all a matter of perspective.

This specific morning, however, I did not feel very lucky as I pulled over and stopped at the parking lot just by our neighborhood grocery store. I was in a hurry to get to work, but the tears rolling down my face made the road impossible to see, and being a risk management professional (or maybe just someone with common sense),

I knew the right thing to do was to pull over and try to calm down before I hit something or someone. I was angry. I was upset. I was disappointed. And the reason was a seemingly trivial exchange with my son's preschool teacher. As I had dropped him off 10 minutes earlier, she greeted us at the door with a smile, but with a raised eyebrow and a very loud voice as she knelt down next to my little boy: "Oh, what a special day this must be!! Is MOMMY dropping you off today? Wow, that sure is something!"

Now, that might not have been so bad if my son had not turned his innocent big blue eyes toward me with a puzzled look. He studied me in detail. All of a sudden, the fact that his mom worked long hours and did not drop him off and pick him up at day care very often was clearly abnormal and something to be concerned about. That moment, my frazzled juggling of a career, being a loving mother and dedicated wife, keeping a clean house, family life, finding time to stay fit, nurturing some kind of hobbies, and being a good and fun friend just came crashing down. I was angry and upset because I have always wanted to be a good role model for my son and wish for him to grow up as a diversity champion, not even flinching when a woman is the primary breadwinner in a family. I was disappointed because I had expected more of a fellow woman. I had expected my son's teacher to be less judgmental and more supportive of a hardworking mother.

I looked at my puffy eyes in the rearview mirror and took a couple of deep breaths. My work-life balance was clearly completely off balance, and I had a sneaking suspicion it would remain that way. What I needed was a new perspective. As I pulled out from the parking lot, my frustration had turned into determination and a positive direction. I was going to shed the guilt and find a new way of looking at things.

Now let me pause for a moment before I tell you how I embarked on a life-changing journey to bring more harmony to my life. Let me put something else in perspective before we continue. I was born and raised in Sweden and have lived most of my life there. Our son was born in Sweden, which makes the backdrop to this story slightly different. Sweden is often cited as the pioneer and role model of a more extensive, successful gender equality policy. Gender equality policy has a long tradition and has become a matter of course in societal and political life. Sweden's family policy is aimed at supporting a dual-earner family model and ensuring the same rights and obligations regarding family and work for women and men. Generous spending on family benefits; flexible leave and working hours for parents with young children; and affordable, high-quality child care are the main factors for success. In addition, Sweden has some of the most generous parental leave laws in the world. Parents are allocated a total of 480 days per child, which they can take any time until the child is eight years old. They can share these days, although 60 are allocated specifically to the father. And they are entitled to receive 80 percent of their wages (although this is capped at a certain level). As a result, Sweden has the largest proportion of working mothers in the European Union.

After having spent three years in the United States, I have realized how incredibly fortunate I was to become a mother in Sweden. I stayed at home 11 months (which, and I almost hesitate to share this, is considered pretty aggressive and career focused!). My husband then took over and stayed at home 9 months before we put our son in day care. The beauty of the model is that employers are just as likely to get impacted by the hassle of having an employee out on parental leave whether the company hires and promotes a woman or a man. It is a powerful equalizing factor. And by the way, yes, it is absolutely a hassle when an employee is out on parental leave. I will never forget when a member of my team came to share the exciting news that she was expecting, and my immediate reaction wasn't one of joy, but instead I blurted out: "Oh no! What are we going to do without you!?" The irony is that I was eight months pregnant at the time, and all she had to do was to look at my tummy to make me feel like an idiot. The employer perspective is always a little different! But in Sweden that perspective very rarely includes a female employee not coming back after having had a baby because almost all do.

With all this said, there is one thing that remains the same for working mothers in the United States and Sweden. The feeling of guilt and stress because of the divided attention between work and family. That draining feeling that you are not giving enough, doing enough, and being there enough for your family.

When you make up your mind to redefine yourself or change your perspective, it takes a deliberate effort, and it is not easy to know where to start. Generally speaking, the first place to start when you want something to change is by taking a good look at yourself in the mirror. I realized that increased self-awareness was a good first step to identify and address some of my work-life pain points. I will admit it was difficult to concede to, but looking back it is quite clear that I was a control freak. And it polluted every aspect of my life! It has taken me focus and lots of effort to change, and if I am perfectly honest, I still fall back into old habits from time to time. Let us just say that I am a recovering control freak. But, generally speaking, I am more relaxed, so much better at delegating, and less concerned with *how* things get done as long as they get done.

My fellow perfectionists will sympathize with how stressful it was to let someone else take over a project at work, when I knew exactly how to deliver on it, down to the very detail. Or at home, how I cringed when delicate spring asparagus was served on a Thanksgiving platter featuring a crazy-looking turkey. And don't even get me started on school potlucks, when I came home from work late the night before just to slave away in the kitchen until 2 A.M. to be able to bring homemade cinnamon rolls. Being a perfectionist will slow you down and at times make you absolutely miserable. Even though the brief moment of happiness when you live up to the Photoshopped image of perfect and something is done exactly the way you want it can be rewarding, a more even and sustainable level of everyday contentment and joy beats it time and time again! Another benefit of letting go of control a little is that you invite and allow others to develop. It also makes it easier to enjoy the present, and you will likely come across as a nicer person. I know I did. These days I am perfectly content as long as all family members look reasonably presentable, and at work focus more on the end goal and the ability of getting things done than anything else. If you want to make a change, take a look at your habits and decide not to let perfect be the enemy of good. Giving up on that hopeless quest of being a super-mom and flawless parent was one way for me to start enjoying raising our son without feeling guilty, anxious, and exhausted. And just know that at the next parent-teacher potluck mixer, it is perfectly fine to put forward a large tray of cupcakes, and if someone asks you if you baked them, smile big and say: "I made the frosting!"

My second big insight was that there is not one single path to success, and whatever it is, you can't walk it alone. It is absolutely crucial to develop a strong support network, both at work and at home. Some have a partner they can rely on, some call in parents or siblings for support, and others find an awesome nanny. Asking for help and making sure you have support is a sign of strength, not weakness. One very successful female executive I know made the creative decision to hire a personal assistant instead of a nanny. Her kids are old enough to more or less take care of themselves, but her personal inbox was overflowing with e-mails from school, sports teams, and the drama club. Having an assistant help her reply to e-mails, put reminders in her calendar, and take care of things that needed to be prepared or bought has taken a great deal of pressure off her. She can focus on work and spending quality time with her kids, instead of having to chase down a couple of boxes of tissue and hand sanitizers for school when she has a moment to spare.

There is not one solution that will work for all, and we can help each other by being respectful and supportive of the different choices we make. A friend of mine is adamant about how important a principle it is to take care of household tasks like cleaning, laundry, and ironing yourself. I love her dearly but could not disagree more. Outsourcing domestic chores can end up saving so much time and energy that the cost is well worth it. Let go of the pride and get a housekeeper! There are few things that beat coming home and finding every single room in the house clean. At the same time! Our family from time to time also relies on a company that provides fresh ingredients for a weekly menu delivered to our doorstep. We can enjoy home cooking without having to plan or shop for groceries.

You have to define what success means to you—understanding, of course, that the definition will likely evolve over time. Moreover, I believe that it is important to have a shared vision of success for everyone at home, not just for yourself. My husband and I spent time on developing a clear understanding of what success means for our family, and we now work together toward that goal. Our relationship offers both of us opportunities that we might not otherwise have had, and maybe in a slightly unconventional way. When I was approached about the incredible opportunity to move to the United States, he made the difficult decision to leave his job to be able to come with me. Our son was five years old at the time, did not speak a single word of English, and needed a lot of support to make the transition to a new environment and culture. It would have been nearly impossible for me to take a step up the career ladder and take on this incredibly exciting and rewarding challenge without my husband's willingness to put his own career on hold and take on a different kind of challenge. Looking back, I am pretty sure he has no regrets. In three years, our son has transformed from a shy Swedish boy to one of the more confident all-American kids I have ever come across. While he is busy with school, friends, and sports, my husband has had the opportunity to write a cookbook, set up a micro-brewery, take beekeeping classes, and play golf. Lots of golf. He lives a life many can only dream of, and at the same time fills the crucial role of family logistics manager. He has always been my best supporter and cheerleader. On occasions when I come home deflated, exhausted, and ready to give up, he always reacts the same way. He will give me a brief moment to reflect, and then look at me with his sweetest, most loving smile and say, "Honey, you would really be the worst mother and wife if you didn't have that job. I know you love it. You know you love it. Now get back in the saddle." And I know that he is right every time.

The final big change that I introduced in my life was a total energy waste moratorium. It is incredible how much time and energy we waste on things we can't control, or just thinking of how guilty we feel. I realized that I had been wasting so much energy thinking about everything I hadn't managed to get to at work as I was brushing my son's teeth or reading him a bedtime story. And then the next day I would feel bad about not spending enough time with my son, as I was trying to focus on a conference call at work. It is a really poor equation with no winners. It is critical to make the choice and be intentional about being fully present in every moment, whether you are spending time with your family or if you are at work. It is not easy to avoid getting distracted, but limiting multitasking as much as possible and trying to be laser-focused on what is going on right here and right now has helped me reduce stress levels and feelings of inadequacy. Some parents actually get to spend most of their days with their kids, and yet they are never fully present! It is all about perspective and deciding what matters to you.

Thinking of the importance of deciding what matters reminds me of a story a close friend shared with me years back. She had been under a lot of pressure at work for an extended time period and came home every night tired, frustrated, and snappish. It reached a point where her two kids almost avoided her because being in her presence just was not enjoyable. When she arrived home one evening, absolutely exhausted after having been away on a demanding business trip, she shoved the door open, threw in her roller bag, and stepped into the kitchen, letting out a big heavy sigh. Her teenage daughter who was sitting at the kitchen bar, looked up at her and said, "Mom. We don't deserve the leftovers." That was a transformational moment for her and a life lesson that helped her identify a real pain point in her life. She realized her priorities were completely off, and that she had not spent enough time thinking about a good definition of success for herself or her family. I have carried this story with me for the past number of years, and to this day every time I pull up in the driveway outside our house I take a deep breath and think to myself "no leftovers!"

You may wonder if these lessons and reflections have translated into my own leadership, and I really hope they have. I have worked hard to develop flexibility and at this point quite honestly think that my team members should be able to work wherever, and whenever, they chose so long as projects are completed on time and goals are met. It is much more important to focus on results rather than on the number of hours spent in the office. I want to believe that I am supportive of my employees' personal issues, and I try to share my own priorities outside work to serve as a role model. I strive to achieve a sustainable work environment, with a happy and healthy culture where people are loyal, thrive, and work hard because they are passionate and committed. It has to be okay to want it all, and you can have a fulfilling, successful career and still enjoy enough quality time with your family. But it takes a little bit of planning, some intentional choices, a willingness to compromise, and recognition of the fact that you cannot do it alone.

Chapter 7

Dirty Glass Ceilings

Yvette Connor
Managing Director
Insurance & Risk Advisory Services
Alvarez & Marsal

I started actively working when I was 12 years old. I sweatily worked bicycle delivery in the morning and afternoon as the neighborhood local newspaper girl. I moved on to low-paying part-time jobs in high school, and slightly better-paying part-time and full-time jobs throughout college. I accelerated quickly up the professional ranks, all the while diligently and passionately applying myself to the pursuit of work excellence. In one of my first professional jobs, I received a 12 percent annual raise. I asked my manager, "Is this a good raise? What are the normal ranges for an annual raise?" Looking back at this, I am struck by my overwhelming naïveté. Nevertheless, over time I came to strongly correlate my career success and my satisfaction, based on my performance and results.

My career was fast paced—a quick vertical escalation into management and leadership roles, fueled by my interests in problem solving, innovation, and risk strategy. I needed big goals, dynamic workspaces, and lots of active problem solving to keep me interested in my work. I challenged myself by pursuing a graduate education, convincing myself that performance alone was the paragon for achievement. Nothing else mattered. This approach paid off handsomely. I regularly was identified as having "high potential," and I had success with both male and female managers. I was endorsed and promoted to senior management by the time I was approaching 30. During this time, I simply could not understand the occasional cocktail party, business dinner, or conference speaker reference to a "glass ceiling." Where was this often-maligned "ceiling"? Perhaps this clear, delicate, amorphous barrier had slowly faded into obsolescence with the rise of my fellow Generation X colleagues? After all, many of us Gen X'ers lived through both John Hughes movies and dual-working families. Many of us were also the first in our families to attend college. So, frankly, over time I came to the conclusion that this ceiling simply must be rare or nonexistent. There was no ceiling in my work environment, ever—until the exact moment there was.

There is a fundamental truth in business—one that arguably applies to many professions and both sexes. When we are young, we are naïve. Young working professionals often do not tactically understand the professional roads they are driving on, including how to anticipate roadblocks and then change course. The flip side of youthful naïveté is dream making. Youthfulness brings energy and ideas, and youthful new views change and mold the future of our world. Youth inspires the current regime to do more and to do it effectively and more nimbly, while also bringing forward innovation and know-how. The challenge is that while they are quickly racing down the road focused on a dream-enhanced target, they are not necessarily taking the time to anticipate the exact type of road that may face them. For instance, the journey may have an incline and require more effort, or it may decline and require braking; perhaps the path becomes curvy and requires some tight maneuvering, an object emerges and creates damage, or you need to pick up passengers and achieve consensus among participants and stakeholders. In the worst case, the journey is severely affected by weather, with fog, snow, rain, or mud slowing down forward momentum and creating driver frustration. Over time, navigation challenges begin to take on new personal shapes and sizes. Young professionals, particularly women, begin to develop a burgeoning level of self-awareness of being a "woman in business." As such, women begin to experience and respond to items that are competing with their careers. These competing twists, turns, and roadblocks are commonly rooted in solving for career versus work-life balance; remaining a technically proficient performer versus taking risks and embracing becoming a leading resource for strategic planning; and staying silent versus solving for obscure and often politicized decisions. One of the common roadblocks encountered by both men and women involves political maneuvering versus living in your truth.

For women, work-life balance is a frequently discussed challenge, especially as female professionals traverse through their childbearing years. During this childbearing/family development period, which can last decades (20s, 30s, and now even into the 40s), women encounter tough decisions about family, career, and bandwidth available to manage family time and competing working priorities. This seems to be more of an issue for women than for men. Why? There are many more men today who are "stay-at-home dads" while their female spouse continues to work. Many households are also dual-working households. Again, why are childrearing years such a challenge for working women, and do we manufacture glass during this time period?

In my third managerial job as a risk management professional, I began to think about scenarios involving one of my key female employees. She was dynamic, young, and hardworking, married, and had no children. My concern was that she would have a child, take time off, and I would be hard-pressed (and stressed) while she was out on maternity leave and may struggle to keep the risk management boat from taking on water. Looking back, my experience tells me that men likely have this same concern, and it regularly applies to high-performing young female employees. The U.S. work culture has led us to believe that having children likely makes employees less effective and that family responsibilities (as a mom, in particular) create a drain on performance. Kids get sick, the school calls and someone in the family has to pick up the child; there are sporting events, parent-teacher conferences, and a myriad of activities and parenting responsibilities that come into play. Women—not men—are perceived as the "responders" to these items. Why? I suggest it is because we women have manufactured this piece of the looking glass, and in doing so we essentially became a direct competitor with our U.S. business environment. This occurs in the face of modern technology and employment laws that often push for and protect options for maternity leave, working at home, flexible work schedules, and providing opportunities to use your grit and work your (butt) off without necessarily having to have that same (butt) in a seat, in an office, all day.

The glass ceiling actively begins to creep into the picture during these family development professional years. Let's be clear, though—both women and men manufacture the glass ceiling, but these years are where women manufacture it more. It is not intentional, but it is innate and instinctive for a woman to naturally choose family over work. At the same time, while women are finding their way through the difficult converging paths of family and career, men are tightening up their "club membership" rosters.

The "boys club" membership has many unwritten rules. Highlights include an ability to be constantly available, networking during a golf game, early morning starts, able to meet after work for drinks, similar "male" experiences (played sports, fraternity), reliving the childhood dream (money, fast cars, beautiful women), and being married to an attractive woman that other men can envy and admire—as being married to an attractive woman suggests a man has both confidence and sexual prowess.

Women have a club as well. However, it is much more loose and opaque than men's. Women's club rules seem to vary by professional level. Lower management levels share common themes around men, climbing the ladder, family activities, faith, community, and planning/participation in employer activities (softball team, clothing drives, young professional groups, work-related professional networks). As women advance in their carrier, club rules begin to change. Examples generally include topics such as gaining visible professional power (senior management titles, public speaking, and board seats), participation in management of professional associations and leadership roles in their professional networks, negotiating with men, firing men, leading substantial teams, building strategic plans, raising successful children, staying physically fit, and being able to stay in the overall professional game.

Along the way, as we move through various membership club conversations and subtly qualifying events, the professional road helps us with self-actualizing and working through competing interests, essentially building our experience repertoire and gaining a real-time, informed awareness about how the business world actually works. This an important point because we gain professional experience and awareness by working through the turns and twists and solving for better solutions, more so than simply barreling through to another job or remaining stagnant. Gaining experience in how to formulate solutions and work well with others is a true enabler of success. Over time, we actively and directly apply this experience to our careers. We learn, adapt, stumble, and learn again. Experience helps us understand what we could not understand in our youth. Experience also begins to help us understand that there are barriers and roadblocks, some of which are fair and surmountable and others that are obscure and difficult to see or solve. Over time, we may identify and understand the particular nuances built into these challenges. Some of these nuances are different and unique to women; others are not. Nevertheless, our experience begins to help us "go around" or, perhaps, wait out the weather. The difficulty is that when you cannot anticipate a specific type of roadblock, solutions are not self-evident and the solution becomes difficult to navigate. The result is that you just hit the roadblock—head-on.

I always wanted to be in control of my career, which meant setting my own speed limit, changing lanes whenever I wanted, and pursuing fast goals. So I took innovative risks (my vanity plate is "BINOV8V"), and I was always open to new jobs presenting me with strategic opportunities and more money. Yes, money, and let's add on power, which is perhaps the ultimate prize. Power allegedly gives you full control over your professional destiny, or we think it does. Ironically, during my youthfulness I did not understand how a professional journey might actually occur. I believed in the purity of hard work, know-how, innovation, problem solving, and leadership skills, believing these would carry the day and continuously propel me forward. For many years, my beliefs held true. What I did not see or recognize was this—as I gained experience and advanced further in my career, over time I was gradually entering into the glass manufacturing phase. This is a subtle and dynamic shift, not obvious to many of us. It is a time during which men and women both manufacture glass. Then, the men rise above the glass production floor, while women buy the glass products thinking (naïvely) that these products are harmless, iridescent objects—not realizing, in actuality, the glass is a professional kryptonite.

In my role as adjunct faculty at the University of Colorado Denver, School of Business (I teach in the risk management and insurance program), I have the pleasure of watching youthful ambition play out every semester. My students regularly inquire about my career, wondering how I achieved my goals, built my professional brand, and obtained my success, and, frankly, curiously inquire if an education is the key to the ultimate ride. In my conversations with them, I see how their delightful and inquisitive personalities correspond with a whirlpool of innocence. They do not yet understand the fuller realities about progressive and modern pathways for managing their success. Their vision is clouded, not unlike mine was many years ago, and they are enthusiastic to race down their professional roads, holding their master's in business degree and accelerate their professional dreams, while seeking their "best job." Throughout this experience, I notice an interesting pattern between groups of my students. My female students, who are often some of the brightest and hardest-working students in my classes, are often the least confident. They hold back. They ponder. They question. This is in stark contrast to the male students, who have little to no hesitation in taking risks on their assignments, speaking up in class, immediately connecting with me on LinkedIn, or even asking me for a job.

I encourage all of my students to be their best educational advocate and self-champion, and to use the information I share and teach them to grow and develop their risk management careers. Often, I will spend time playing psychologist or mediator for students or student teams who are struggling with effective and productive team participation, including managing confrontation with their peers. This is an imperative issue because during my class we work through a semester-long group assignment that involves playing a war game. During the game, you have to creatively solve risk management issues, while negotiating with your peers (other teams) and responding to their feedback, which could consist of the answers "no," "yes," or "maybe." I stress the game environment by forcing the game into a zero-sum decision-making framework as we move toward the end of the semester. I note interesting team trends that I can identify based on three factors:

- Blended teams, (B+) either female (F) or male (M) leaders
- Female lead, all-female team (FE)
- Male lead, all-male team (MA)

Blended teams (B+F) demonstrate higher levels of collaboration. They problem solve, often extensively and arguably a fault. These teams are slower to get to their final or even interim decisions than blended teams But aren't you talking about blended teams here?(B+M).

FE teams tend to hesitate to take dramatic steps, proceeding in a more strategically incremental fashion, and are keenly focused on how their answers impact other competitors within the game environment.

MA teams demonstrate rapid decision making and tend to be over-confident, aloof, and not fully informed. They make obvious mistakes and often lose sight of the specific deliverable.

MA teams regularly draw first blood in the game and most often are the perpetual aggressor in a deal-making transaction, even in dealing with a female-led team. They will, however, ask for forgiveness from F or FE teams, typically after bludgeoning them first with aggressive risk strategies. It is important to note they take on the MA teams with equal gusto. However, they often get strong block responses from the MA teams and will back off.

It is important to remind the reader that I am referring to a war game, which means there is only one winner. Playing the game wisely involves using risk management fundamentals, specific class lessons, and external research, all executed through a risk-based decision-making approach. Putting this all together over the course of 16 weeks earns you a better grade. The variance in team behaviors—including risk taking, aggression, direct/indirect tactics, confrontation, negotiation, and problem solving—I can compare between the team types is interesting to me. It also corroborates with mutual glass manufacturing, including the subtler components involving the decisions F and FE teams allow B+M or ME teams to "get away with" and whether the game begins to feel personal to the team leaders. I keenly observe the game to see how and when women chose to be the aggressors and risk takers and what motivates them to identify and navigate a roadblock, change to a new course, stagnate, or, in some cases, quit (and sometimes drop the course).

Thinking back to my own MBA days, I was often the female lead on a team. Not always, but often. I enjoyed the pressure of going to nose to nose with an opponent and leading my team members, both male and female, to a successful outcome. To me, we were all one team, one set of equals. I had never experienced any inhibitions suggesting I was going to be any less successful in business or school performance than my male peers. My male (and female) counterparts became good friends; many still are today, and there was mutual respect during our educational journey together. I worked hard and graduated at the top of my class. During school, I never hesitated to do what it would take for our team (or myself) to get the A—extra work, extra diligence or research, tutoring, practice tests, asking for assistance, and many hours of dry runs prior to team presentations. I ran for office during my MBA (first year), and when it was all over, I was elected commencement speaker for our MBA class. Afterwards, I was president of our alumni association for few years. My MBA alma mater had provided such a great experience and contributed to my career enhancements that I wanted to give back. I never—and I mean never—saw my sex as a hindrance to my success, while in school or afterwards.

My risk management career rapidly accelerated following my MBA. I graduated from role to role, moved companies a few times, and learned from some of the best in the business. The latter favorably colored my view. When you have a great boss, a great leader, or a great teacher, you flourish. So long as someone is coachable (teachable), and willing to understand their shortcomings, advancement opportunities are usually ripe. This held true for me, and I was very lucky, and honored, to have some fabulous bosses, mostly male but a few females, helping me chart the path of my career. My salary was nearly doubling every five years, on average. I was accelerating my brand in the professional marketplace. I was also making mistakes, making bad hires, recouping from bad management decisions, owning my mistakes, learning, and adapting. This effort was paying off, along with a fair amount of eating humble pie. In particular, my male bosses were very instructive, and when I asked for ideas or help, they told me how to best advance my career. One, in particular, told me to quit and take another job I had been offered or risk his calling me a fool.

I applied for my first risk manager job when I was in my late 20s. I was young and considered myself a long shot for the job. Amazingly to me at the time, I was their candidate of choice. Prior to applying, a friend had called me and let me know that a local, large organization was hiring. When I read the job description I thought to myself, this is my dream job. It was complex, challenging, and involved some topics I knew well and some that I had absolutely no clue about. I knew I wanted that job, though, and more importantly, I knew I could quickly learn and excel at the job, so I applied. The interview process was long and grueling. When I received the call and the job offer, I was a bit panicked. Why? Because I thought that I had perhaps oversold myself and I questioned my ability to fulfill my potential in a fairly visible risk management position. I met with my current boss and let him know about the offer. He had been a tough but effective mentor, and he was thrilled for me. He told me to take the job, immediately, and not look back. Here's why. My boss informed me that in order to advance and succeed, I had to stretch and become uncomfortable. I needed to leave my day-to-day technical expertise, my hard-earned comfort zone, and move into the realm of senior leadership. I could do this only if I accepted new challenges. I would run a bigger team, much bigger than I ever had before, and learn to navigate through a large, complex company. He said it would be the safe choice to say no, and the leadership choice to say yes. I did not negotiate the salary. I accepted the initial offer and was thrilled to be making substantially more compensation. In hindsight, I have no idea why I did not negotiate the salary. I cannot imagine, today, not negotiating my salary.

As the years rolled by, I refined and eventually built, from scratch, various risk management departments, enjoying the diversity of solving for business solutions across domestic and international companies. After a decade or so, I decided to return to school to pursue a second master's degree, this time one with a dedicated focus on risk management. This was arguably one of the hardest choices I had to make in my professional career. I had an eight-year-old daughter, and I was already traveling extensively for my job, working with global risk management clientele for a large risk consulting/insurance brokerage firm. I convinced my husband that the year 2008 changed the face and function of risk management. The result was dramatic and immediate, with new regulations, approaches to modeling risk, solutions for underwriting risk, and, certainly, new approaches for risk management altogether. In order to be at the top of my risk management game, I needed to update my skill set and challenge myself to compete on a newly paved road. Between working full time and attending school, I had zero work-life balance. It was one of the most difficult experiences of my professional life, even though I loved every class, the school, my school colleagues, and the results I was seeing in myself professionally. After graduating, I threw myself back into my day job, full of new ideas and, not unlike my MBA students today, anxious to take my career to the next level.

A global consulting firm approached me about joining and leading their enterprise risk management specialty group. By this time, my salary at my current employer reflected my expertise, my accomplishments, my leadership skills, and my entrepreneurial success in driving change and delivering results. As such, the salary negotiations this time around were materially different than what they had been when I accepted my first risk management position. I had equity and cash bonuses that had built up value within my current employer. I also knew that there would be substantial risk in moving from my existing employer and deeply rooted management position into a full-bodied global consulting position where I was accountable for not only project results but a P/l (profitability results). As such, the compensation needed to align with the strategy and the risk. In this instance, I knew my BATNA (best alternative to a negotiated agreement). Simply stated, if I did not receive a salary commensurate with the risk I was assuming and that covered my currently earned cash position, I was not going to take the job. It would create a bad taste in my mouth to leave good money on the table—on top of demonstrating foolishly bad decision making. I provided financial analysis, profitability forecasts, summaries of my current equity and cash holdings (in current employer vested/unvested plans) and requested full compensation for all amounts already earned or owed. The negotiations were extensive and, at one point, I absolutely planned to launch my BATNA and stay in my current job position.

When all was said and done, the new compensation package was acceptable. My soon-to-be new boss mentioned he hoped he never had to do another compensation negotiation like it. Perhaps this foreshadowed the path I was agreeing to walk on. I resigned my current position and excitedly began my new career in full-time enterprise risk management (ERM) global consulting. As time progressed, I began to realize that I was seeing and experiencing some new discussions. I had gone from merely being in a man's world to actively trying to live and survive in a man's world. I participated in meetings that were clouded in club-ish innuendo, unusually offsetting to me in a lack of synergy between transparency and strategic direction and my ability to be in control of my leadership environment. I began to notice I was missing what I had always found so refreshing in many of the business environments where I had worked—a wholesome respect for those sitting around the table, and communication that just felt honest, fair, and collaborative. These changes were inconsistent, coming and going like weather patterns. I asked myself, where has this change come from? Is it new? Is it just me? Have I become more "sensitive" as I have gotten older? (This may seem odd and out of place, but this is where my mind went.) Why haven't I had this happen before? Of course, it was not new. I had just finally slammed into something that I never realized really existed. My femaleness was an activated, material factor for the first time in my career.

The barrier's blunt force stopped me cold, creating disorientation and discouragement and reducing my confidence to a former shell of my former self. I found myself second-guessing my reasoning, my logic, my perspective, my leadership approach, and eventually my success. I was losing confidence, and fast. This was completely new territory for me. I realized the reason I had not foreseen this coming was that the ceiling was clouded and dirty—you had to get close enough in your respective career path to hit it, before you could actually see it. There was little room for course correction or avoidance because I had been inexperienced in knowing what to look for and how to manage around or through it.

I began to realize I was going to have to get creative, very creative, in finding solutions that would help me succeed in my new environment. This included where to expend energy pushing back and where to let things simply pass by me. I found myself a male executive mentor and sponsor—someone who did not look at me like he wanted to sleep with me, recognized my professional talents, and understood my weaknesses. Perhaps most importantly, he taught me political savviness, including how to relate to differing (often male) perspectives within my current environment. My mentor reinforced the importance of mastering emotion and being politically astute. Generally speaking, this is not easy for women. Our female communication and group-think style are all pretty well established by the time we survive middle school. However, my mentor gave me ideas and I learned about solutions I could apply. This was similar to finding a bottle of Windex. I could then clean the ceiling and move forward, clearly seeing where to break it wide open.

I learned to not let comments, behaviors, or a lack of fulsome communication get under my skin. It took time, and without good coaching from both my former and current mentors, and my husband, it would have been very difficult to strike the right balance and move forward. From the beginning, the importance of good mentorship has held true. It can never be underestimated and must be sought and practiced constantly during one's career.

So how do we solve for identifying and "going around" or through this obscure glass ceiling? In the absence of wisdom, will the ceiling naturally break apart as Generation X and the Millennials begin to take command of companies and change the culture for themselves and for others? Or perhaps the sheer volume of women moving into the workforce will create enough pressure upward that the ceiling will crack and begin to give way. If it's the latter, and therefore more of a numbers game, then we are well on our way to success if we can keep women in the workforce longer term, and not leaving or accepting lower positions during family rearing years. Today, women comprise a substantial component of the workforce, much more so than in the 1970s or even the 1990s. This bodes well for the numbers game. Last, but not least, there is the additional factor of a woman U.S. president possibility. Is it time for this to happen, with the people's choice for U.S. president finally being a woman?

Time will tell, but all of these factors suggest we may be closer to substantial progress than we think. Perhaps this decade may truly be the decade of change, opening the way for many women to gain experience, quickly move into leadership positions, and perhaps more easily find solutions for work-life balance that will keep them in the workforce longer. In the meantime, fasten your seatbelt and get ready to drive. You've got an exciting, challenging road lying ahead of you.

Chapter 8

Integration: The Key to Happiness

Janet Pane
Head of Market Relationship Governance
Willis Towers Watson

"Don't let the perfect be the enemy of the good."

From Voltaire to Shakespeare to modern self-help blogs, we see this sentiment repeated over and over again across the ages. So what does it mean? I take it to mean that in our zeal for personal and professional excellence we have to be careful not to overdo it. With today's busy lifestyles and stressful workloads, it is easy to become overwhelmed. How do you ensure that your unique essence, your authentic self, is protected and preserved? When should you be content with what you have accomplished? Overachieving in every area of our life comes at a high cost, and I suggest it is time to take it down a notch and reexamine what is really important. What makes you happy?

I have personal experience in perfectionism. With the exuberance of youth, I believed that having it all was easy. My career was soaring, my family was a constant source of pride and joy, and I was doing really good and important work at one of the largest global insurance brokerages in the world. I was tired most of the time due to the grueling hours, but the adrenalin kept me going, until I began waking up at night with crushing chest pains. A trip to the doctor confirmed that my heart was fine—it was the pace that was killing me. My pursuit of perfectionism led to exhaustion and a high level of anxiety, which was having a devastating effect on my health. This was a literal wake-up call to reevaluate my goals, life choices, and my approach to work.

I had to accept that my previous approach to balancing both my private and professional life was not working. It was leaving me tired and anxious, unable to serve my family and clients from a calm place where I could use my talents to truly listen to and respond to their needs. I needed a more holistic approach. That was when it hit me. I realized that I am only one person, one whole person who should not split herself in two any longer. Integration of my professional and personal being was the key—not balancing two spinning plates. I knew I had to stop compartmentalizing my needs and learn how to plan my day differently. I needed to start making better choices in order to lead a more fully integrated life.

Choices

Living life in the modern world on your own terms requires introspection. We all make choices in life, and the choices we make every day will lead each of us down a different path and result in different outcomes; regardless of how similar we may be in other, more visible and measurable areas of our lives. Your choices are largely guided by your values, your interests, and your drive. Defining your own personal values can be a very interesting journey. But it will help set you on your own authentic path to achieving your goals. To take back control, ask yourself some fundamental questions. For instance, is it more important for you to be relaxed and to have more free time to pursue your hobbies and interests, to live richly in a deeper sense but perhaps have slightly less material wealth than others? Or is it more important for you to work harder for bigger rewards, sacrifice your personal time, and lead others in order to effect great change or even make the world a better place? Both are equally valid and respectable approaches to life. Are you living by your own values, and have your choices helped you achieve your goals? Each person has a different drive and sense of what they owe to the broader community. That sense may change over time as you grow and gain more experience. Understanding what makes you feel satisfied, centered, and happy is important to goal setting and making decisions that allow you to take back control over your life and career.

My nighttime wake-up call drove me to write down my personal goals in life. I highly recommend this activity even if you believe you know them. Ask yourself, how well do your daily commitments—the things that take up the majority of your time—match your goals and interests? I was surprised to find that my day-to-day activities were out of alignment with my goals and core values. For instance, good health was one of the top personal goals I had identified for myself; yet I had failed to establish a regular exercise routine, often telling myself I didn't have the time. Upon reflection, this was one of the sources of stress for me. I knew I should be taking better care of myself and failing to do so left me feeling guilty and anxious. This period of introspection also reminded me that at my core I am a very creative person. I majored in theater at school and loved the arts, yet that facet of me had been completely swallowed up by my obligations at home and at work. All that perfectionism takes a lot of time!

Following my visit with the doctors, I made a choice to sit down and take stock of what had to change in order to create some much needed breathing room in my life and time to pursue other passions. I was lucky because at just that time I came across a study conducted by McKinsey called the Leadership Project. It highlighted a fact we all know, that fewer women occupy the top leadership seats despite the same high levels of intelligence, education, and commitment as men. The study aimed to find out why. They focused on five leadership attributes they call the Centered Leadership model, which they believe enables and sustains leaders in an ever increasingly complex world. The five themes of Centered Leadership discussed in the article are Meaning, Framing, Connecting, Engaging, and Energizing. The conclusion of the study was that while many people possess a few of these leadership qualities, the most successful leaders excelled at all five.

I was intrigued by this, and reflecting on these five attributes I thought about my own journey.

Meaning. I know that both my home and work life filled me with a sense of purpose and meaning. Providing for my family and serving others is what truly motivates me. I have a great respect for the industry I work in and believe it exists to offer people peace of mind by providing for them when they or their companies are faced with disaster or loss. Within my company I set out to solve problems and create a work environment that is generous and supportive in helping both the company and my colleagues achieve their goals. When I think about meaning as a leadership quality, I believe it goes back to my point on making value-based choices that lead us to a place where we feel we are doing something important and making a difference.

Framing. Positive framing is a way of viewing potentially negative situations and finding the opportunity within them to create positive action. One door closes, another opens type of thinking. I have encountered too many people who waste tremendous amounts of energy focused on the negative. They tend to take situations personally and allow it to paralyze them, rather than taking the necessary steps to move past the event and onto a successful solution. I was lucky enough to be born an optimist and view difficulties as an opportunity to make things better. Regardless of your natural disposition, all of us have the ability to develop this capability. If you lead people, mastering positive framing is a critical skill to keep teams motivated and focused on the goals. I have found in my career that the biggest achievements often stem from a point of failure. So face the challenges with a smile!

Connecting. The benefit of working in the insurance industry—and for that matter, the same company—for many years is that you get to know everyone over a long period of time and know what each of them is working on. One of the characteristics I am known for is that I love connecting people and helping others find a network. I also tap into these contacts if I need to find an expert, so the concept of reciprocity is big when you think about your network. You have to be willing to give freely, secure in the knowledge that it will come back to you tenfold. Building a strong network of allies and mentors is essential to your professional growth, as they provide insight and opportunities that you are unable to see for yourself. I became aware that while I was very good at connecting others I was not very good at keeping up with my social network on a more personal level. Who had time to socialize? I had a wonderful mentor who was also my boss at the time, and he was the first person to tell me that while I accomplished 120 percent of what was expected on the job, I needed to start making time to be more social with my colleagues. At first, I thought he was crazy. With so much to do shouldn't he be telling everyone else to work harder rather than telling me to slow down a bit and spend social time with the team? Once I stepped back and thought about what he was telling me, I understood the wisdom. What a gift! I realized I was wasting time trying to achieve perfection when increasing my impact by interacting with more people would provide a better result. With time at a premium I had to build social networking into my schedule. That was when I developed the habit I now call "three phone calls and a lunch." Each week, I try to schedule one social lunch and make three phone calls to colleagues that have no business need involved. Research shows that while women tend to have deeper relationships with people, the circle is much smaller than men who create wide but shallow networks. The result is that men naturally tend to have a wider sphere of influence and have a greater ability to enlist people to their cause. I realized that a concerted effort to increase social interactions and to volunteer more would create more followership for my work than the extra two hours spent perfecting a report.

Engaging. Nike's slogan "Just do it" is my career motto. My interest in how things worked, in finding creative ways to do things more effectively, and my experience in problem solving led me to take on different projects and new opportunities throughout my career. I have always been open to jumping into new challenges and believe this quality has been a key ingredient of my success. Men are more likely than women to jump into a new role without possessing all of the skills, knowing they will pick it up on the job. Never hold yourself back from trying something new because you may not be perfectly qualified. I have relied on the subject matter experts on the team to provide the detailed knowledge I may not have possessed when moving into new roles. By acknowledging the value of others, you provide them an opportunity to shine and a path for their success as well as your own. Frequent interaction with your team builds a sense of common purpose, and I want to relay one of the tips a former colleague of mine shared on how he makes sure he stays engaged with the people on his team. Recognizing that at around 3 P.M. every day he needed an energy boost, he got up to get himself a can of Coke; he decided to use that time to walk the floor for 15 minutes while he drank the soda and engage with his team informally. Sometimes the conversation was focused on a project they were working on, but other times it was about a recent vacation or family event. For the team members not sitting in his physical office, he would make a 5-minute phone call just to check on them and to say hello. As a result, his teams loved him, and they felt he was a very engaged manager and was in touch with what was going on. Think about small changes you can make to achieve the same result.

My goals have always been focused on creating constant improvement, so I have moved outside my comfort zone for most of my career. That is where I believe real growth occurs. You have to have the courage to take risk if you expect to achieve great things. Go out and create the change rather than wait for it to find you. Be bold and audacious, and be flexible in your approach. Revise direction when the facts suggest you should, and don't be afraid to speak up when that is necessary.

Energizing. Looking at energy as part of the five Centered Leadership attributes, it hit me that this was my Achilles' heel. I have always had a lot of energy, but I had to acknowledge that there were areas of my life that created a drain of energy. I have always been self-directed and self-motivated, but I was pushing myself too hard. Harder than anyone I reported to could possibly push me. I wanted to be perfect in accomplishing all my projects at work, but as a result, I was beginning to experience burnout. I needed to find things that boosted my energy. This was the missing ingredient. In order to sustain the pace and demands of my daily life and the increasing responsibilities, both at work and at home, I knew that I needed to address the exhaustion and find a way to energize myself. Leaders need to maintain the resiliency required by today's demanding business environment.

Changes

With a fresh perspective on my goals and the understanding that I needed to manage my energy in a new way, I set out to define new routines for myself. I identified the main things that nagged at me and drained me. I wrote each item down and began to check them off my list. Next, I began posting my goals in a place I could see them each morning and reviewed them at the end of each week to make sure that at least some of the activity was driving toward my goals. The sense of relief was immediate.

I read a book a number of years ago on getting things done at work, and it touted the idea of immediately placing work requests into one of three categories for action—Do it, Delegate it, or Defer it. I decided to try this on for size. I began thinking about my colleagues and realized that delegating more to the people on my team and building their skill sets was not only key to their personal development but would also help me focus on the most critical items and allow me time to think more strategically.

This realization led me to evaluate all of my relationships at home and at work. Was I taking on too much of the burden? Where could I use more support? I began making requests and taking steps to improve my partnerships. Create more balance—more free space in my schedule. Once you look at where you spend your time, you will be surprised to find there are things of low value that you really should stop doing. Or you will find a way to reduce the amount of time spent on them. For instance, if you find you spend a lot of time each evening getting dinner ready, you may decide to cook double portions and immediately freeze half for future meals, cutting your effort in half.

I had a lot of fun identifying time wasters in order to make room for the things that would boost my energy. Small changes paid big dividends. Below are a few of my changes, but you will need to find what works best for you.

- I created more productive hours in the day by negotiating work-at-home days. This saved hours in commuting time each week. I split that saved time between work and family. This was harder back when I made this change, but today most business environments are much more open to remote workers.
- Have an agenda for every meeting and hold people to it. I hold crisp 45-minute meetings, not hour-long meetings, and use the extra 15 minutes to check e-mail or write the follow-up notes. Creating breathing time between meetings allowed me to become more organized; no longer did my approach to meetings feel like speed dating! By building some free space into my schedule I was able to collect my thoughts and show up more fully present and engaged.
- Schedule stressful meetings—those that drain your energy—in the morning so you get them out of the way while your focus and energy are still at their peak. Don't schedule these types of meetings back to back or even on the same day if you can avoid it, as they zap your energy for the entire day.
- Reserve time for yourself in your schedule. I now book 30 minutes in each day for what I refer to as "pop-up sessions." Use this time for all the people who drop by just to ask you a question or would like a minute to discuss something with you. Tell them you are free to meet with them during the time you reserved, and this will eliminate a series of interruptions during the day that can derail your own focus and deliverables.
- Do not constantly check your e-mail. It pulls your focus. Unless you are awaiting something urgent, set times during your day to read your e-mails and respond.
- Pick up the phone and speak to people instead of using e-mail as the sole form of business communication. Conversations will reduce the number of e-mails that fly back and forth, and they help build relationships.

- If you can manage, hire people to complete the weekend tasks like the lawn, housekeeping, laundry, and shopping. Sometimes it is less expensive than you thought. Your time is precious, and you need rest in order to restore your energy.
- Lay out your workout clothes the night before so they are waiting for you when you wake up. Even 15 minutes of exercise in the morning will help prepare you for your day. You can do the other 15 minutes when you get home. The point is that even a small amount of exercise is better than none, so stop waiting for the perfect workout morning and just do something to get your motor running.

Compensation

Make sure your partners in life, both at home and at work, share your goals and respect what you bring to the table. This is a critical step on the path to integrated happiness, but it is also a key component in the area of compensation. This is a lesson my mother taught me at an early age, and the wisdom of it has guided me in selecting my partners carefully. I was fortunate in my career to attract good bosses and mentors who understood my value. Even the tough ones taught me something that I carried into the next position. It is important to understand that your success is tied to theirs. When they look good, the entire team looks good. Good results for the company means there is more income for shareholders and employees. When you tie your goals to the company goals, you have a better chance at improving your compensation.

I believe in servant leadership, and that has shaped how I operate. Servant leadership is a philosophy and set of practices that builds better organizations, enriches the lives of individuals, and ultimately creates a more caring world. I have always given more than I expect in return. I believe in creating a generous work environment and identifying and exceeding the needs of colleagues, customers, and communities.

When it comes to the wage gap between male and female colleagues, I don't believe there is a magic bullet. There are, however, topics to avoid when asking for a raise. It is always best to avoid comparing yourself to others, or using other people as a benchmark of what you should be achieving—to quote King Lear, "That way madness lies."

Always approach the promotion and raise discussion prepared to identify your value in both qualitative and quantitative terms. Be able to identify how you contribute to the success of the company and why a raise or promotion is justified. Too often, I have had members of my team come to me and say that they deserve a raise because of the years on the job or because it was unfair that someone else appeared to be getting something they were not. Also, while it may be true that your personal bills are increasing, that is not a great approach to the raise discussion. Companies prefer to focus on the value you bring to them to help them achieve their own financial goals.

My commonsense approach over the years has been to do the job that was asked of me, ask for the jobs I wanted and even create roles for myself when I saw there was a need, and to articulate the impact and value of what I achieved. This last part is very important. If you do great work, but you keep your head down and don't engage, who do you think will notice? Ask for the pay increase and articulate why you deserve it! Companies need leaders in all shapes and sizes. It is a proven fact that companies with diverse leadership outperform others. So whose responsibility is it to make sure that all talent is recognized, promoted, and compensated fairly? I would suggest the responsibility lies within each one of us. At the board level, companies need to review pay disparity and implement governance procedures to eliminate it. I hope that when my two daughters come of age and join the workforce, there is forced disclosure of these issues and the pay gap will be a thing of the past. Until then, each of us as individuals need to use our platform to promote others, as a rising tide lifts all boats.

Closing

I have started to live life on my terms in order to navigate and succeed in a busy world. Integrating the various aspects of my life and keeping my personal goals in mind has paid me huge dividends in both physical and emotional happiness.

Reviewing the three "C's"—Choice, Change, and Compensation—has led to the realization that perfectionism is overrated. Please stop trying to be perfect and remember the wise words of Confucius, who said, *"Better a diamond with a flaw than a pebble without."*

Chapter 9

Women on Boards

Terrie Pohjola
Board Member, Thrivent Trust Company

W omen have successfully chipped away at the glass ceiling for the past few decades. However, there is one area where progress has been more limited—female membership on corporate boards of directors.

Board gender diversity is generally defined as women representing 30 to 40 percent of outside board members. I have been fortunate to have career experience with two great companies that have already achieved this parity: SECURA Insurance and Thrivent Trust Company.

At SECURA Insurance, 30 percent of the board members are women. According to David Gross, SECURA President and CEO:

> The role of women has become so critically important in all aspects of our business. We look at gender diversity at all levels, from our board of directors, to my executive team,

to our leadership team, and for all associates. We currently have 30 percent of our board members who are women, and although we do not manage to a percentage, we know that this diversity helps us so greatly as a board and as a company.

At Thrivent Trust Company, 50 percent of the outside directors are female. According to Jesse Ostrom, Thrivent Trust Company chairman of the board, president, and CEO:

> While I don't naturally see or define board members by their gender, as I reflect on the topic, I realize that given the collaborative nature of the board environment, this balance of female representation on the Trust Company board has served us well. In my overall board experience (having served on six boards) I've been impressed with what strikes me as the unique contribution that seems innate to the female board members. The level of commitment and emotional connection that women bring to boards I've served on has tended to generate richer discussions and debate than I suspect would have happened on an all-male board. The quality of these discussions— as one would expect—often generates more effective outcomes than would have happened without the gender-balanced input.

In Europe, where the strongest increase in female representation on boards has taken place, many governments have passed legislation mandating female board representation or set suggested targets. This has no doubt influenced positive change. During a six-year time frame, the number of European companies in the Credit Suisse Research Institute report *Gender Diversity and Corporate Performance* who had at least one woman on their corporate board increased from 50 percent in 2005 to 84 percent in 2011.[1]

Unfortunately, gender parity on corporate boards is not widespread here in the United States. In California, a resolution was passed directed at board composition of publicly held companies. Senate Resolution 62 calls for three female board members on boards of nine or more, two female board members on boards of five to eight, and one female on smaller boards. However, progress elsewhere has been nonexistent. Catalyst, a leading nonprofit organization with a mission to accelerate progress for women in workplace inclusion, analyzed the Fortune 500 companies in 2013. Sadly, the study showed only 16.9 percent of board seats were held by women—unchanged from 2012. In both years, 10 percent of these companies had no women on their board, and less than 20 percent had more than 25 percent female board members. And only 25 percent had three or more women directors.[2]

Yet evidence abounds pointing toward the greater success of those companies that have female board members. For example, Credit Suisse conducted extensive research on gender diversity and its impact on investment performance in their August 2012 study. Credit Suisse indicates:

> In testing the performance of 2,360 companies globally over the last six years, our analysis shows that it would on average have been better to have invested in corporates with women on their management boards than in those without. We also find that companies with one or more women on the board have delivered higher average returns on equity, lower gearing, better average growth and higher price/book value multiples over the course of the last six years.[3]

Catalyst also performed a study in 2007, which showed that the companies with higher percentages of women on their board outperformed other companies 53 percent on return on equity, 42 percent on return on sales, and 66 percent on return on invested capital.[4]

Despite the fact that gender diversity matters, global progress toward this target is actually slowing down. Ernst & Young recently conducted research on the impact of gender diversity on business disruption. They found that about half of the companies interviewed believed they could achieve gender parity in the next 10 years.[5] Yet, according to the World Economic Forum's 2015 report, this level of diversity will take 117 years to achieve at the current pace of change, an increase of 37 years from the 2014 report.[6]

This inequity is astounding, considering the fact that women represent a majority of the investment decision makers in the United States due to their longer life expectancy. And it is estimated that nearly 75 percent of all U.S. household spending is controlled by women.

So why aren't more corporate boards seeking gender diversity? While I do believe recruiting methods currently employed by corporate board nominating committees in the United States generally do not favor women, I also feel that women are not as often setting their sights on a seat at the boardroom table and thus not actively preparing themselves for this role.

While driving gender diversity may be an uphill battle, female professionals should consider seeking a corporate board position. Since you are allowed and often encouraged to continue your current job responsibilities, serving on a corporate board provides the opportunity to display your leadership skills at an additional company. And, as I have experienced, you can continue your board service into your retirement years.

Preparing for a role as a corporate board member requires a long-term plan. Take these five career steps to be "board ready."

Step 1: Join a volunteer board. The first step is easy—join a local, nonprofit board. Women do have a strong representation on nonprofit boards, and lack of board experience isn't a roadblock. I started serving on not-for-profit boards when I was in my early 30s and continue to serve and provide advisory services to area nonprofits.

Nonprofits are always looking to add great leaders with good connections. Choose an organization that matches up with your passions. As you become more familiar with the organization, work your way up to more responsibility on the board by accepting roles as a committee chairperson or officer. On average, after about one to two years on a nonprofit board, I felt confident in accepting chairperson or officer roles and gained these positions on each nonprofit board I served on.

As a board member, you are a representative of the organization throughout the community and you will definitely be judged for the performance of the organization. Be a good promotor and help the nonprofit to expand its influence. Keep your eye on oversight, and be prepared to spend the time to learn the organization's financial situation. I served as interim executive director at two organizations that experienced financial setbacks, and the board members at these organizations had to put in many extra hours to help get the organizations back into the right light in the community. While this is good business experience, it is not one most would relish.

Your experience on a nonprofit board is a valuable addition to your resume and a source for references when applying for a corporate board seat. Many C-level executives and board chairs serve on nonprofit boards. You can demonstrate the skills most valued—leadership, collaboration, strategic vision, and insight—to individuals who are in a decision-making position on their corporate board.

Step 2: Take advantage of board training programs. Most local community foundations or United Ways offer training to new not-for-profit board members at minimal cost. Take advantage of these programs to help you learn more about the unique leadership demands on board members. The additional training will increase your effectiveness as a board member and expand your knowledge of corporate board governance in the process.

Or if this type of training is lacking in your area, you could advocate change to improve the situation. Recently, I led an effort to expand nonprofit board training in my community after area leaders recognized the gap in available training and materials locally. A web site had been developed with a myriad of resources and references on all aspects of board governance. Yet the local nonprofit leaders realized this was only the start. Efforts are now under way to offer more frequent training opportunities on a regular basis.

Step 3: Broaden your skill set. As a board member, you have ultimate responsibility for all aspects of the corporation's performance. While everyone brings specific strengths to the table, you really need business acumen across all areas of corporate governance. Look for an opportunity in your current company to demonstrate your leadership skills in an area outside of your discipline.

As a certified public accountant (CPA), my emphasis was in finance, but I also took on leadership roles in information technology (IT), sales, and program business during my career with SECURA Insurance. This broader experience was crucial in gaining my corporate board position. I was fortunate to have the support of SECURA senior leaders, who accepted my role in their division based on my leadership skills and were very patient in allowing me to learn the required technical aspects of the jobs.

"We encourage women to first serve on nonprofit boards and to accept rotational opportunities within our company, for we know that will also help our high performers to succeed in any role inside or outside of our company." Gross commented. "Terrie is a great example of fearless acceptance of rotational positions, which has made her an even better board member for any prospective company. She has been both my peer and also worked under me. I respect her talent and leadership so very greatly."

Displaying experience on your resume in a variety of disciplines will demonstrate your ability to learn new things and effectively lead without detailed hands on experience. This is truly important as a board member's role is to strategize and oversee—not question day-to-day management. Believe me, no board chair, president, or CEO wants a board member who is too focused on management-level decisions. They are looking for a visionary with a new and different perspective who can guide them through high-level corporate challenges.

If your current corporate environment doesn't have a formal program for cross-functional leadership, maybe you can start one. I have found that most insurance companies are open to providing special leadership opportunities for their high performers. Or you can gain similar experience by accepting a different role as part of the nonprofit board you join. Volunteer to serve on an additional committee outside of your area of primary expertise and focus on gaining further understanding of this new discipline. As a CPA, I served on the finance and/or audit committees, but, I also served on other committees such as human resources, marketing, and special events in an effort to expand my knowledge and experience.

Another method to expand your background is to complete educational courses outside of your current area of expertise. When I decided to pursue my master's degree, I chose to enroll in the environment science program and graduated with an emphasis in environmental economics. I utilized my learning and knowledge to establish SECURA's Green Committee, which drove environmentally friendly efforts for the company. I also developed their first sustainability vision statement as part of the company's strategic plan.

The end result of your cross-functional experience is to demonstrate you are a well-rounded leader, not a silo thinker with tunnel vision of just one aspect of corporate governance. This part of board preparation will likely require the longest time frame to complete, so be patient and choose your opportunities wisely.

Step 4: Seek a board mentor. As you embark on your mission to become "board ready," seek out a local woman leader who is currently serving on a public board of directors. Ask her advice and assistance in pursuing your corporate board seat.

The best place to start is a woman leader who has served with you on a nonprofit board. Or talk to another leader who serves with you on a nonprofit board and works in an organization with a female board member. Ask him or her to introduce you. It is advantageous to start with someone who has observed your board interactions firsthand and so can critique your performance as well as provide advice on best practices moving forward.

While women board members are in the clear minority, I am confident you can find someone close by to work with you on your board readiness. I live in a small city in Wisconsin, but, there are a number of area women CEO's and executives serving on corporate boards. I was fortunate to be referred to a retired female CEO currently serving on the board of a local bank. She described her experience in seeking board roles, the successes and the challenges she faced.

First, she recommended joining two organizations advocating for women board members: Women in the Boardroom and Women Corporate Directors.

Women in the Boardroom is a membership organization focused on preparing women for corporate board service.[7] According to Sheila Ronning, founder and CEO, "Women in the Boardroom evolved over the years. It started 14 years ago before the issue was the hot topic that it is today. A mentor encouraged me to develop an event that educated women about corporate board service—what is the job of a corporate director, what happens behind those closed doors, why serve and how to get a seat at the table. Over the years, I saw a demand from women who aspired to serve on corporate boards to have a map to the boardroom. Women in the Boardroom evolved into a membership organization that focuses on preparing women for board service and helping experienced directors gain additional seats."

Depending on the level of membership, individual membership benefits include access to webinars and other training materials, assistance in creating your board portfolio, board coaching, notifications of board openings, and a matchmaking program that connects members to companies for prospective board openings. I chose to join as a VIP member, which also includes events to meet other VIP members who are also seeking board positions. Interaction with peers in this arena helps to expand your network and connects you with individuals who can provide more advice and mentoring.

Many corporations are joining Women in the Boardroom as well to offer these great services to their high-performing female professionals and promote better gender intelligence within their own boardrooms. "The idea that men and women think differently is nothing new," states Ronning. "But, the concept of corporate boardrooms using these differences as a way to improve business is relatively uncommon. However, more and more companies across North America are seeing value in the concept of gender intelligence. This notion embraces differences in the attitudes and behaviors of

men and women, works to understand and accept these varia-
tions, and uses it to improve board director relationships. With
gender intelligence, the different ways men and women interact, solve problems, make decisions and communicate are realized and appreciated instead of tolerated."[8]

I also qualified to join Women Corporate Directors,[9]
which requires its members to serve as a board member for
a public or large privately held company over $200 million
in annual revenue. The organization has chapters around the
world, and membership is linked to a specific regional chapter that holds regular events. The chapter meetings are another
great opportunity to network with some of the most influen-
tial female board members in your area.

Second, she recommended that I prepare a board portfolio,
which includes a board profile and a resume (often referred
to as your curriculum vitae). The profile is an easy-to-read
document of not more than two pages that tells the story of
your board preparedness. The board profile will be the primary piece to share with your network contacts and serves
as your introduction for those who are responsible for the
board vetting process. I utilized the services of Women in the
Boardroom's professional board coaches to refine my board
portfolio. "We ensure our members have a board portfolio that highlights their skill set for board positioning," states
Ronning.

And finally, my board mentor pushed me to move forward
with step 5 of the "board ready" process—promoting myself
as a prospective board member.

Step 5: **Advertise yourself.** My board mentor told me, "It's not who
you know, it's who knows you." Stay in close contact with your
network of peers who have firsthand knowledge of your leadership ability. I had secured my corporate board seat with Thrivent
Financial Bank (now Thrivent Trust Company) via referral from
a former colleague who knew my background matched perfectly
with the skill set needed on her employer's board of directors.

And take the time to meet individually with folks who
are likely to become aware of open board seats. Share your

board experience and target industries. I developed a list of 10 leaders I had served with on nonprofit boards who either were serving on a corporate board or who had strong connections with the board recruiting decision makers. I personally met with each, provided a copy of my board portfolio, and also specifically highlighted five target industry areas where I felt my background was strongest. I created a 100-day plan of meetings and follow-up to maintain awareness of my goal.

I also took advantage of meetings and events scheduled by Women Corporate Directors and Women in the Boardroom to develop a stronger network of director level contacts. "We teach our members how to network their way to a corporate board seat and how to maintain strong connected relationships with boards through our virtual platform. We also connect our members with board contacts included in WIB's Matchmaking Program," Ronning explains.

In following these five steps, your end goal is to become "board ready." Women2Boards, an organization with a mission to bring gender diversity to the boardroom, has a convenient questionnaire on their web site to help assess your current or future board readiness.[10] I recommend you periodically refer to this quiz and measure your progress toward the "board ready" goal.

Securing your first seat on a corporate board of directors will definitely require some serious time and effort. According to Women in the Boardroom, the average time it takes to secure a board seat is from three to five years.[11] And corporate board service will also be very demanding. Women2Boards estimates the time commitment for a public board position to be between 250 and 300 hours per year.[12] As you are developing your board experience and working your network, plan on devoting at least twice that amount of time to the process. When you begin to actively seek a board role, add another 300 to 400 hours per year to your schedule for the search. In my experience, it is like having a second, part-time job in addition to your current professional position. You will want to be fully prepared to set aside the time necessary to effectively accomplish this goal.

Once you are "board ready," you are on to the next major hurdle: the board vetting process. Most board nominating committees maintain a pipeline of potential directors whom they can call upon as finalists once a retirement is imminent or when a board seat opens for any other reason. Your goal is to be on several board pipelines. Below is a description of the most common board pipeline vetting process and tips for effectively surviving this rigorous challenge.

The pipeline process starts with a broad review of potentially qualified candidates. While a number of board nominating committees do employ search firms, most often they start with candidates who are recommended by current board members. In fact, it has been estimated that only 15 percent of all open board positions are filled by a recruiting firm. Here is where your networking pays off! A recommendation almost always ensures your board profile and resume will at least be reviewed by the committee for consideration. Plus, a recommendation is likely to get you to the next step: the initial interview.

At an initial interview, a subset of the nominating committee will personally meet with prospective candidates either as a group or individually, not unlike any other job interview. When I applied for my current board position, I met individually with the CEO and board chair. Their focus was to vet out my background and experience. I also met with two independent board members, who provided a perspective on how well I would fit with the current board personalities and to test my collaborative skills.

When preparing for the interview, take a look at who is serving on the board, their backgrounds and length of service. Be prepared to communicate how your background and expertise will complement the current team. And be sure you conduct an extensive research on the corporation itself—via web site, social media sites, and a Google search. Not only do you want to be highly knowledgeable of the company you may be serving, but you will want to understand any potential risks to or conflicts with your current professional position.

As an independent director, it is of utmost importance to avoid any appearance of conflict of interest. If there is any doubt, it is best to investigate further before you add your name to the pipeline. While I had good knowledge of Thrivent Financial Bank and a broad understanding of the activities of its corporate parent, further research did bring forward a potential conflict with SECURA. I was able to set up a teleconference with both CEOs and corporate legal departments to discuss and consider the potential conflict in advance of my acceptance of the board seat. After this discussion, both organizations agreed the situation wasn't an issue, so I was able to move forward in the recruiting process.

After the initial interview of prospective board members, the successful candidates are added to the board's pipeline and ranked according to the anticipated gaps to fill with the next board retirement. This ranking can change if a board member leaves early. In my case, a board member accepted a new role at a different company, which created a conflict of interest for her, thus requiring her resignation. This is a fairly common situation.

Having a board pipeline offers the board nominating committee an opportunity to fill the position almost immediately with a candidate who has already been strongly vetted. The top candidate will be subjected to an extensive background check before proceeding to the final step. Since boards have a fiduciary responsibility to the corporation's shareholders/owners, employees, and clients/customers, it is exceedingly important to have a pristine record!

Once the background checks are completed, the board nominating committee also remembers the long-term needs when filling any open board position. When I received the call to serve on my current corporate board, the audit committee chair was due to retire in a year. Thus, my CPA background was critical in moving me to the top of the pipeline list. And I had a year to learn from the then audit committee chair before he retired.

The board I would soon join at Thrivent Financial Bank (now Thrivent Trust Company) was unique in that the board chair was female, and board membership was 50 percent female. The resigning director was a woman, and it was important to this organization that gender diversity be maintained. So my gender was an advantage in this case!

As you can tell, securing a corporate board seat does not come easy. In retrospect, I would have started a more active board search earlier in my career—at least a decade sooner—rather than waiting to work in earnest following my retirement. Most board members are in their mid- to late 50s and can potentially serve for 10 to 15 years before mandatory retirement age (often when members are in their 70s). It takes several years to secure a board seat, as the recruiting process usually begins well before an expected board retirement.

One of the toughest barriers I have had to face in my search is my lack of C-level title. Most corporate boards list a C-level position as a requirement for consideration, and unfortunately this does eliminate many talented women from consideration. And it is probably one of the driving forces behind the slow progress toward board gender diversity. Many women of my age group (Baby Boomers) spent a majority of their career hammering away at the glass ceiling and so enter retirement without securing the coveted C-level title. Of course, it is understandable that corporate boards want to recruit the most talented and experienced candidates to fill their seats. And from their perspective, bringing forward candidates with a C-level title is certainly recognizable by shareholders and owners as someone who has more than adequate preparation for their board role.

In my case, I take part of the blame in that I never asked for my VP titles to be upgraded to C-level. Our male counterparts are more apt to ask for recognition and that is one of the female characteristics we need to be aware of and overcome. I am confident that I had a good case for C-level recognition and had I asked, the CEO would have gladly awarded me this title. I feel this concept applies to the board-room, too. As female professionals making our own investment decisions, we should be asking those companies we work for or invest in to place more women on their boards. And for that to happen, more women have to be "board ready."

And while progress is slow, it may be gaining momentum. "I am thrilled with the progress we have seen over the past five years," states Ronning. "I think boards are realizing the need to have diversity of thought at the table. I believe a smart board will have a matrix, the first column should be a list of the skill sets needed on the board. The other columns should be a mix of other pertinent items including gender, race and age."

However, we can't wait around for gender equity on corporate boards to continue to progress at its current slow pace. It is up to us as female professionals to take charge of the situation and become a driving force behind better gender diversity on corporate boards in the United States. John Bykowski, chairman of the board at SECURA Insurance, stated, "I believe every professional man and woman has an obligation to share their talent and experience in their communities by serving on boards, whether it be a nonprofit or for-profit organization. I encourage diversity on boards at all levels to make certain the organization can service our diverse society."

So what are you waiting for? Now is the time to think ahead and plan for your seat at the board table. It is up to all of us to make this change happen. Companies need more women corporate board members! It is the next glass ceiling challenge.

Notes

1. Mary Curtis, Christine Schmid, and Mario Struber, "Gender Diversity and Corporate Performance," Credit Suisse AG Research Institute, July 13, 2012.

2. Rachel Soares and Liz Mulligan-Ferry, "2013 Catalyst Census: Fortune 500 Women Board Directors," December 10, 2013; catalyst.org.

3. Mary Curtis, Christine Schmid, and Mario Struber, "Gender Diversity and Corporate Performance," Credit Suisse AG Research Institute, July 13, 2012.

4. Rachel Soares and Liz Mulligan-Ferry, "2013 Catalyst Census: Fortune 500 Women Board Directors," December 10, 2013; catalyst.org.

5. "Navigating Disruption without Gender Diversity? Think Again," Ernst & Young, 2016.

6. World Economic Forum 2015 Report.

7. www.womenintheboardroom.com.

8. Scott Chase, Ed., "2013 Directors to Watch," Directors and Boards Fourth Quarter, 2013, p. 43.

9. www.womencorporatedirectors.com

10. www.women2boards.com/talent-registry-women-corporate-board/are-you-board-ready/

11. www.womenintheboardroom.com

12. www.women2boards.com/talent-registry-women-corporate-board/are-you-board-ready/

Chapter 10

A Growth Story

Carol L. Murphy
Managing Director
Aon Risk Solutions

I 'm writing this while vacationing with my family in Dublin, having just over a week ago celebrated my 26th year with Aon, 30 years in our industry. My daughter was lamenting the return to school in a few weeks, and I empathetically (or so I thought) related it to my working day in and day out. She replied, "That is not fair, because you love your job!" Indeed, it's true.

I've been blessed and have a number of perspectives to draw from in considering women's advancement in our industry: that of an earnest and optimistic college graduate entering our business, that of a senior-level professional with three kids and a mortgage, that of a leader with colleagues to empower and engage, that of a leader in our company's Women's International Network (WIN). There's a lot of discussion about what our companies should do to promote diversity and inclusion. That is an important conversation. But there's far less said about what we can do to help ourselves and each other grow our own talent, regardless of gender. So that's my focus, and it starts with developing your growth mind-set. My own growth story closely parallels Aon's growth these 26 years. Some stories regarding the lessons learned along my own growth journey follow.

Good-bye Perfectionism

An important lesson that I learned early on was to let go of perfectionism and focus instead on executing positive outcomes for clients. One of the areas that I believe doesn't get enough attention in the dialogue about women's advancement is that delivering superior results for the firm, with excellence and integrity, is still your top priority. In order to keep growing, you need to be able to get the work done! I am a reformed perfectionist now but struggled with working too hard trying to make things perfect early in my career. I occasionally missed deadlines as a result of this extra effort. Some worthwhile projects remained incomplete because they couldn't be done as perfectly as I imagined. Learning from these defining experiences, I'm religious about getting things done right the first time and on time! Now meeting or exceeding customers' expectations both in results and process is a hallmark of my professional reputation.

On a related note, I procrastinated early in my career because I could. I was single and living in the city not far from the office. I could work until midnight finishing a project or work super-long hours including holidays and weekends. One of the learnings that I benefitted from after having three children in three and a half years was to just take care of things quickly and to work at longer-term projects in chunks over longer periods of time. Some people are naturally better time managers than I was early on, but motherhood reformed my sense of time management.

It is also important to speak up to ask the questions that will help you do your best. It may mean asking for additional resources, time, or assistance. Like many women, I had been raised to be a good student, was highly self-reliant, and did most of my work independently.

Moving from that framework into managing multiple client priorities at the same time and relying on teammates to do good but not perfect work is a step of faith in yourself and others. I am often reminded of the mantra: "Don't let the perfect be the enemy of the good."

Speaking Up

Learning to speak up and finding your distinct voice are critical to growth. Speaking up means, among other things, having a respected opinion, being heard, and being listened to. Countless times, I witness meetings where a less experienced team member is the expert on the subject at hand, having done most of the work and research, but fails to speak up. As leaders, we are sometimes guilty of overpowering a discussion and not allowing space for a colleague to demonstrate his or her expertise. My first mentor at Johnson & Higgins (J&H) was an engaging leader and was inclusive. She prepared me for what my role would be in a meeting so I could be prepared to shine. I was shy. If she hadn't made that extra effort, I would likely not have spoken up. If I didn't get the chance to speak up, I wouldn't have developed the level of respect with clients and colleagues that I achieved. I was always part of the team, invited out after work, included in the most challenging and highest-level client meetings. That's what inclusion felt like in my early career. Feeling included, encouraged, and engaged prepared me to keep speaking up and raising my hand for growth.

Speaking up also means raising your hand for new and challenging growth opportunities. Around this time, I was given an opportunity to intern with the only female partner at J&H, Christine La Sala. I will never forget the advice she gave me as a broker with only two years under my belt. She suggested I seek out the very hardest, most difficult accounts to broker, and to raise my hand for those opportunities. This advice was pivotal, and I was given the opportunities to work on teams for the biggest and most challenging opportunities. By learning to negotiate in the most difficult of circumstances, I developed my voice, my "brand" that has sustained me throughout my career.

Difficult conversations are part of speaking up, too. It is important to make leaders aware of your goals and objectives professionally.

Often, you must initiate applying for a promotional position or new role within the firm. Leaders are focused on the business at hand and can't read your mind! Conversations on compensation can be difficult for many women. I find that it is helpful to be prepared and to base the conversation on the value you can bring to the firm. In addition, it is important to be realistic and as objective as possible, considering the big picture of your value proposition to the firm and the firm's value proposition to you.

After getting my MBA, I raised my hand for a promotion with relocation. We were building out our large account practice groups around the country, and I was offered an opportunity to lead the risk management practice in our San Francisco office. Wearing my employer hat, I can see how beneficial it is to the firm to move high-potential colleagues to meet business needs in different geographies. As a colleague, it is a fantastic growth opportunity to go to a new place and more or less start over with a new group of teammates and clients. You have to earn your place on the new team, as the deployment chart doesn't do that for you. This was one of the most important growth experiences of my career, so my advice to the next generation of leaders is to embrace change and have a flexible framework when thinking about geographic opportunities.

Comfort in Ambiguity

One of the critical things I had to learn early in my career was to get comfortable with change and ambiguity. At first, I believed that I was in control of my work and that by doing the right things, I'd get ahead. The risk business that we're in now, however, is complex and getting more so by the day. One of the changes that created ambiguity in my first several years at Aon was a series of major mergers and acquisitions. What was exciting about this growth at the time was the additional breadth of capability, resources, and scale to serve our global clients. As our firm was growing by leaps and bounds, the best aspects of our client-centric culture emerged. By embracing the changes and opportunities that came with this growth in the firm, instead of being fearful and uncertain, I was able to grow by leaps and bounds, too.

Developmentally, my J&H mentor had assigned me to a wide variety of difficult projects and client engagements that were very different than the experience I had prior to coming to J&H. These stretch assignments were very important to my professional growth. I'm still a believer in gaining a breadth of experience in your early career, not specializing too narrowly. As employers, we have an obligation and a challenge to provide those growth opportunities. It would have been more comfortable to stay with what I knew already, but continuing to stretch and grow in different areas was critical to my success.

When my husband and I moved to San Francisco, our team in Chicago enjoyed leading market share in the risk management space. We worked very hard, but there's a certain comfort level that comes with being a leader. You get more business opportunities, and it is easier to win as the firm's reputation is strong. However, in 1999, our team in San Francisco was going through growing pains after several mergers, and we had lower market share there. We were often the "underdog." Being the underdog makes you work much harder to prove yourselves. I've never lost that hunger to win, to work really, really hard to meet customer needs and win with customers. "Listening harder" is one of the aspects of our culture at Aon that has contributed greatly to our growth. So while we are naturally drawn to the "comfortable" experiences, again, it is often those uncomfortable times that make us grow.

External Focus

In my work, external focus means an unwavering focus on our clients' best interests. External focus is closely tied to growth. Shortly after I joined J&H, there was a reorganization and an account management practice was launched. I was nervous about the reorganization, as it brought me a new boss and was different than the job I had signed up for just a few months prior. My mentor's advice was that in times of uncertainty, putting your head down and focusing on doing your best work for clients was the right strategy. She was right, and this advice has sustained me though inevitable bumps in the road. By focusing my energy on the job at hand, I have been able to maintain a growth mind-set and achieve better results for clients. In addition, this focus has given me the clarity I needed in times of uncertainty.

After I had moved to Aon, my original mentor left the business for personal reasons early on. Our brokerage business at the time, Rollins Burdick Hunter, was a much smaller business then. It was an exciting time, as we were growing the firm so rapidly. Because I had always been included and had demonstrated a passion for doing my best for clients, the clients I served were very comfortable with me, and voiced their confidence that I could take on the senior role. One of our largest clients at Aon at the time, Sara Lee Corporation, gave me this opportunity. So the clients were the ones really responsible for my promotions.

External focus also fuels innovation. This has been a cultural imperative at Aon since the beginning but has exploded over the past 10 years. Working on collaborative and supportive teams to develop new content and capability is fun and engaging. Innovation drives the firm's growth and in turn is a great developmental opportunity for you. Champion your own and support others' ideas and projects to bring greater customer value through innovation.

By the mid-1990s, I was leading teams that were successful quite often and we were winning new clients at a rapid rate. I was always drawn to large and challenging new business opportunities and asked for them. One of the most important lessons of my career was that growth is the lifeblood of the business. By asking to be on the teams to grow the business and then winning as a team, multiple benefits ensue. Great exposure and more opportunities follow. Clients advocate for you and refer you to other clients. You keep learning about new client challenges, new solutions, new risks. You gain responsibilities and the trust of your clients and colleagues. Always raise your hand for those growth opportunities.

Learning to Lead

A series of promotions followed, and I learned that growth can be uncomfortable. With much more responsibility at this stage, I went into workaholic mode. I started managing a team in 1994, and this was a huge growth experience. Some of the respected colleagues who were reporting to me were much more experienced than I was. They didn't necessarily trust me at first and may have doubted that I deserved the promotion. That's probably due in part because I was so focused on the clients and the work, that I didn't pay enough attention to my teammates. What I needed to do was develop empathy. I wish I had known then that you need more balance in life in order to be the kind of empathetic person to whom colleagues are drawn as a leader, with whom clients wish to partner. Yes, you need to work hard, but you also need to get up from your desk and spend time learning from and listening to the team. Over time, I did learn this and became a better mentor and leader. I am thankful to those many successful colleagues who were patient with me during that time where we were all learning so much. Speaking up for others and helping them grow is the most rewarding career opportunity you will have.

Another critical step in my learning as a leader occurred after I stepped out of my comfort zone in brokerage to take a leadership role in Aon's newly minted program that supported the growth of women in insurance called Women's International Network (WIN). We had formed multiple business resource groups to benefit a wide range of colleagues under Corbette Doyle's leadership as our chief diversity officer. Corbette had become one of my mentors when I had previously worked with her on a client engagement. When she approached me about leading our women's network for the Chicago region, I was initially reluctant. I had three very young children and a demanding day job already. More importantly, I wasn't sure what I had within me to contribute to this important effort. But Corbette was very passionate and persuasive, and she convinced me. This was another very rewarding experience in which I've learned so much through service of others.

In my MBA coursework, we did most of the projects and case studies as a team. Several of our courses were combined with the school's executive MBA program in Europe, then based in Barcelona, and our teams were blended with the global teams. Working with others who had completely different backgrounds and experiences to find solutions to business challenges was eye opening! I learned firsthand that diverse teams developed better solutions and that these teams solved problems I could never have solved on my own.

Twenty years after leading my first team, I was asked to serve as a facilitator for Aon's Engaging Leaders workshops that we provide to leaders of our teams. This has been a tremendous gift and opportunity to keep learning by sharing experiences and ideas with other leaders. Your career is a marathon, not a sprint. There will be stretches where things aren't clicking as much as you'd like, where there are missteps. There will also be stretches where it feels like you are firing on all cylinders, everything is going well, and you are having fun. If you are creating a fulfilling career where you feel that high level of engagement most of the time, you are very blessed. I've found that when I'm feeling so engaged, it is because I'm completely focused on clients. So feeling engaged makes your work better, which makes you more successful, which makes the firm more successful. Engagement is a key building block of growth.

High Expectations

At times throughout my career, I've listened to feedback that my expectations for others were too high. I have appreciated the feedback but truly believe it is important to hold yourself, as well as the rest of the team, accountable to high standards. My experience is that when teammates expect the best of you, you do your best work. I'm thrilled when teammates ask me to serve on client teams and expect me to do my best. When clients have an expectation that you can solve a difficult challenge, you work harder to rise to the challenge. When Corbette expected that I could take on a leadership role with the WIN, I rose to the occasion.

At the same time, I have learned that you can be "hard on the issues" while being "soft on the people." This learning took me some time, and I have learned to have more empathy and to listen better to teammates' challenges and concerns. I am still working hard at this.

Mentors and Sponsors

Another great blessing has been many mentors and sponsors through-out my career, several of whom I've identified herein. This is something that the organization can and should encourage and facilitate. But it is also important that you ask for help, ask for advice, and identify relationships to build or strengthen.

I was nominated to Aon's charter group of Strategic Account Managers in 1997 and this was an incredible growth opportunity. I was privileged to have earned a leadership role on the team for many large and important client and business opportunities, and great exposure ensued. My sponsor at the time really helped me gain perspective, and I began to focus more clearly on the goals of the firm, moving from the "trees" to the "forest." Having a strong sounding board in this sponsor was critical. I learned so much about the realities of the business. He also nominated me for Aon's sponsorship for my MBA program at the University of Chicago, another great growth opportunity.

I have many mentors now, both inside and outside of Aon. Through working together to meet client needs, as well as working together on initiatives to advance women in the industry, I've developed strong relationships with senior industry leadership both inside and outside of Aon. I also enjoy many peer mentors, whom I often call on for advice regarding both business and career challenges. Networking was something I didn't fully understand earlier in my career. I had good relationships but didn't always reach out to find solutions that were mutually beneficial. While you need to stay focused on your "day job," it is critical to your growth that you get out there and get to know others and hear different perspectives.

Rules, Written and Unwritten

It is really important to observe the written and unwritten rules and when you can step outside the guidebook to help a client and grow the business. There are unwritten rules in every organization, and it helps to be paying attention. An example of a gap between the stated policy and unwritten rules I notice with respect to many organizations involves business attire. Many companies advertise business casual environments and even "jeans days," but a casual observer would notice very few of the leaders dressed casually. I think you need to be careful in those environments to dress as you would like to be perceived. If you wish to be perceived as a leader, you need to dress as the leaders dress. Of course, there are many companies where even the leaders dress in jeans on the jeans days, and that level of alignment sends a clearer signal.

With respect to the known rules, you need to discern or ask for guidance from leadership as to which are critical and which are really just guidelines. There are times when you will break some of the "guidepost" rules in order to create a winning solution for your client or your company or both. It is important not to do this in a vacuum but to seek advice from mentors and leaders if you feel that the right path is outside the guidelines. Also, there can be legitimate uncertainty or seeming contradictions between well-intentioned guidelines, for example, those coming from different practice groups or business units.

The Juice

Many who have worked with me more recently are surprised to learn that I started out in this business as shy and introverted. A large part of my growing up experience was to learn to be strong and proactive in my communications. This occurred over time, as many mentors pushed me to do more industry presentations, in some cases to large groups. Authenticity is really important. As an example, I'm not good at telling jokes. I appreciate it when others do it well but I can't adopt that style. It is best to be yourself, but striving for your best self. My answer to the jitters is to be well prepared. The more you can prepare and anticipate, the more confidence you will have in your presentation.

As another piece of advice on communications, make your important conversations verbal and direct to those they are intended for wherever possible. I find it getting frustratingly common given how time strapped folks are to avoid these direct conversations and rely on articulate and meaty e-mail exchanges. I know you can feel that you are more articulate in writing and may not have the confidence to say the things you are expressing verbally. Allow that to force you to consider if you should be saying it at all, or using the same tone or directing the message to different people. As a leader, I can tell you that long e-mail exchanges in the absence of supporting conversations may be perceived negatively.

It can pay dividends to be strong and original as a negotiator also. I know not everyone's career involves full-time negotiating as mine does, but everyone's day-to-day life and work involves negotiating. It is very helpful to not only be prepared in your own position but to anticipate the counterparty's position. I've observed over the years that some of the most valuable and creative deals I have been able to negotiate for clients included aspects that other brokers wouldn't be willing to even ask for! There can be a view that the other party would never agree to it so why bother? This is a dangerous path to mediocrity and the antithesis of a growth mind-set. Have the courage to develop a well-prepared and informed argument for the very best win–win solutions. Again, this builds your confidence and your reputation. As you develop your strong voice, others will come to expect it from you, and the negotiations will get easier as a result. You may even be able to build upon your successes.

Several years ago, I began an engagement with a client that was tougher in many ways than any I had handled previously. This has been a tremendously rewarding experience since then, but working as this customer's advocate brought my voice to a much stronger place than it had ever been before. Shortly after we were working with this client, we were asked a very difficult question by the customer. It would have been easy to dismiss as not being our job to answer, one of those we'd be embarrassed to ask others. I considered who I could ask and then reached out and got an answer straightaway. A high-level colleague started saying he couldn't believe I had "the juice" to have solved the customer's question. I am appreciative that he made me realize I had grown up as a negotiator. I always thought "juice" was something that other people had—people who were usually men who were older than me.

Assume Positive Intent

A theme we've worked on for several years at Aon is assuming positive intent. This has been very helpful guidance for me to remember when in any disagreement, whether with a colleague or someone on the other side of a negotiation. Most everyone is working to do their best and have good reasons for their positions. Seeking to understand both sides can be incredibly valuable to gaining trust and understanding and establishing an agreement. Leaders take initiative to make things better. Understanding the positive intentions of others helps us challenge ourselves to continue to try to innovate or find solutions that make things better.

The Dream

I often tell friends that my family represents the "American Dream," but we know that it is really a human dream, the world around, to continue to improve for the sake of our families and future generations. Both of my parents were able to attend four years of college, the first generation in their families to do so. My father was only able to attend because of the G.I. bill, as he came from poverty but had served in the Air Force. I was encouraged to keep learning, that I was never done learning. This growth mind-set pushes me to seek the solutions to problems, to seek to make things better. It also helps me adapt to changes and uncertainty because I can view them as a new challenge to learn through.

It Takes a Village

I would be remiss if I didn't address work-family balance after mentioning my having three kids in just over three years. It was a challenging time, but my children are the greatest blessings of my life. Being the main breadwinner of the family, it did not make sense for my family for me to work part time. I was also one of those people that would have put in full-time hours for part-time pay if I did. My husband was absolutely supportive during this time. As you can imagine, being home overnight with babies and toddlers aged six months to four years while I was traveling for work was no small feat! My advice for others going through this phase is to rely on others. I was able to find wonderful nannies who became truly part of our family. Aon and my clients were wonderful to me during this time. I did moderate my travel and hours and was able to work from home on occasion. Many clients agreed to lunch appointments so I could travel there and back in a normal workday. I am so thankful to those who understood my family situation but allowed me a work framework where I could still contribute at my best.

Circling back finally to the organization's efforts on diversity and inclusion, I can testify that inclusion worked for me. Inclusion drives engagement. Engagement drives better work for customers. Engagement drives innovation. Better value for customers and innovation drive growth. Growth fuels the firm's ongoing success. The success of the firm brings success back to the colleagues.

Chapter 11

What If …

Linda Lane
President
Harbor Health Systems

O vercoming that little voice in your head, leaning into vulnerability and harnessing the power of courage and worthiness.

"What if?" Two simple words, just six mere letters, yet some of history's most compelling achievements were launched by them. It is a deceptively simple question that quickly can grow into a juggernaut of an idea like "what if we could harness fire?" Or "what if we could fly?" I recently came upon these words and they resonated deeply inside me, right in the center of my chest. The first, a concept of facing something unknown, dangerous, frightening. Something that through trial and resolve was ultimately conquered and controlled by man. The other, a seemingly fantastical concept that captured the curiosity of man throughout the ages; men who tried and failed time and again to put action to their dream of flight, yet whose perseverance achieved greatness. And it was the power of two little words, what if, that set the tone of this message and touched me in a way that gave me explicit permission to be curious beyond what seems imaginable and set aside those two little bearers of frozen dreams: fear and doubt. Being curious can be a nerve-wracking experience for one simple reason. To be curious you have to be brave, and to be truly brave, you have to be vulnerable, and to be vulnerable, you have to allow yourself to be truly seen and to believe that you are enough. You have to be open to hurt, to judgment, to being afraid, and, more importantly, you have to stand in the face of it, nose to nose, and no matter what the outcome, even something you weren't expecting and didn't want, to be resilient.

Our modern history is filled with incredibly successful women who demonstrated vulnerability, faced their fears, and in spite of failure, ultimately achieved greatness. Oprah was publicly fired from her first television job as an anchor in Baltimore for getting too emotionally invested in her stories, which is the core personality trait that has endeared her to millions. J. K. Rowling was a single mom living off welfare when she began writing the first *Harry Potter* novel and went on to be the first billionaire author. Despite being broke, divorced, and depressed, she continued to push. In her words, "It is impossible to live without failing at something, unless you live so cautiously that you might as well not have lived at all—in which case, you fail by default."[1] Lady Gaga got dropped by her record label, Island Def Jam, after only three months; upon receiving the news, she "cried so hard she couldn't talk." She rejected her critics and believed in her talent. Today, she has six Grammys and is worth a reported $59 million. Vera Wang failed to make the 1968 U.S. Olympic figure-skating team. Then she became an editor at *Vogue,* but was passed over for the editor-in-chief position. She began designing wedding gowns at age 40 and today is one of the premier designers in the fashion industry, with a business worth over $1 billion. She might not have excelled in her first venture, but her belief in her own self-worth allowed her to stretch her curiosity and to dream in another direction.[2]

What all these women have in common is that they took risks, stepped away from what was comfortable, asked what if, and put themselves in situations where they risked being judged. And if they failed, they didn't stop, they continued on their path, asked a different "what if" question, dialed up their curiosity, their courage, their vulnerability, and in the end, were resilient to the push and pulls from the external world.

It is the stories of these women, their drive and openness, and my encounter with "What If" that allowed me to dig into my own story. I recently realized that my story is a story of the pursuit of vulnerability and resiliency. A story of being truly seen, risking the uncomfortable, and being brave enough to explore my curiosity and just try. However, this is not just a fable, not just a story, it is the zigs and zags of journey. A story has a beginning, middle, and end. But a journey is a process, the fabric that weaves together the progress made from one place to another. A journey is not about the end; it is about the experiences in between. My journey has been an evolution of curiosity and courage. Of stepping away from what I perceived to be the path to success, and of finally leaning into what was uncomfortable as I allowed myself to be vulnerable and authentic to the true me, as I continually discover who the true me really is and continues to become.

From the time I was young, I was in pursuit of perfection. My mother was a nurse and represented the ultimate of female achievements. She had a meaningful job when very few women were in the workplace, raised four children, and had a long and loving marriage to my father for nearly 55 years before he passed away. My father—a man who influenced my life, teaching me honor and commitment, working more than 30 years serving the Boy Scouts of America. He worked hard, provided for us, and encouraged us at every turn. I can still hear my dad's voice saying: "Get your nose out there, little girl" as he nudged me into the big and sometimes worrisome world. My brother and my sisters pursued their dreams, set their course, and achieved success; my middle sister is a certified public accountant, the other a real estate broker who now owns her own agency, and my brother is a comedic juggler who found his way to Las Vegas, writing, producing, and performing. As the youngest, I watched their achievements, and it set a course that I felt compelled to follow. My family is my strength and my courage. My whole life, all I've wanted was for them to be proud of me. I wanted to be strong and fearless and take on the world.

In my attempt to ensure that my family was proud of me, I fell into a common misperception: the trap of perfection. The trap of perfection pushed me to think that I needed to be perfect to have others be proud, which is blatantly untrue and just part of my own perceptions. In my pursuit of perfection, I found myself constantly facing fear and self-doubt. This is the trap, since perfection is impossible, at least the perfection that you have in your head. I actually choose to not follow some of my dreams for fear of failure, of making mistakes, and of disappointing others. You know that moment in your life, when you feel you are right on the edge of joy and accomplishment but then are overcome by vulnerability? Your internal voices start yelling loudly how you are not enough and you become vulnerable and are thrown head first into fear? It's interesting, it's shocking, and it can rock your foundation and make you pull back. Society instills perfection in us from the time we are very young. We are taught to get good grades, win the best awards, and get the best raises and promotions. In essence, society gives us the gift of struggle right from the beginning. And if that's not enough, the more you achieve the more you feel compelled and almost accountable to not just be better, but to be perfect and the trap of perfection springs.

Therein lies the problem and the basis of my journey—the trap is sprung and you don't even realize it.

Throughout my life, there have been countless times when I have set my sights on a goal, did the work to get me there, then reached that critical moment and let the fear that I was not perfect get in the way. I'm not talking about giving up part of the way there, I mean, I got all the way to the finish line and stopped. I literally handed back what I had earned. I convinced myself that I did not stack up against those who had come before me—that I was not good enough.

Throughout our lives we come face to face with opportunities. Sometimes we're ready for them and the choice is easy. Other times, the opportunity, the one right in front of us, finally in our grasp, seems frightening and we have to make a choice. Do we face that fear head-on, or do we attempt to outrun vulnerability and uncertainty?

A theme began to emerge in me. I found myself choosing only those battles that I knew I was perfect enough to win. If there was a chance that I might attempt something and fail, or be less than perfect, I found a way to avoid it, to run, to navigate around the opportunity. I began to wonder why this theme was showing its face at different points in my life. Maybe only choosing winning battles is part of growing up. Maybe it is different between men and women. As a culture, certainly Western culture, we perceive men as brave, strong, and fearless. They don't back down, are confident, and when given an opportunity, they are prepared for success. The mythology is that men are unflinching, don't seek approval, and lead with strength, putting emotions to the side. At least I used to believe the trap of perfection had a gender bias, that women felt it more intensely than men, but now I am sure that men experience many of these same feelings of the trap of perfection, that the trap is not gender specific.

As I moved into my adult life and began to expand my career, the pursuit to achieve stayed with me. I set my sights on commercial real estate, earned my broker's license, and achieved every professional designation in my path that would lead me to being the best. But as I continued to rise and advance, so did that fear of failure and rejection. I attempted to mimic the confidence, commitment, strength, and decisiveness that I believed to be present in the successful individuals with whom I worked so closely. My industries of choice—commercial real estate, insurance, and health care—just happened to be dominated by men, and thus, by default, they were primarily male characteristics that influenced my learned behavior. I believed that if I were accomplished, then I would be deserving and therefore the path in front of me would be easy and without error—perfection, in fact. I do feel that this is part of the gender bias of the perfection trap. As women, we so often believe that we have to be accomplished, perfect in essence, at something *before* we are good enough even to try and step into the ring. Charles Craver, a George Washington University law professor, wrote, "Males tend to convey more confidence than women in performance-oriented settings. Even when minimally prepared, men believe they can 'wing it' and get through successfully. On the other hand, no matter how thoroughly prepared women are, they tend to feel unprepared."[3]

As young women of our generation, we have watched and learned from our surroundings in which we believe that we can't have any limitations to be successful. Perhaps it is a perception of gender bias, perhaps it is simply our resistance to being vulnerable and not acting like men. Perhaps it is a feminine trait to form an outer shell that cannot show any weak spots for fear of somehow looking less than deserving of an opportunity to try.

One of the most relevant examples of this for me came after almost 10 years of hard work as I was offered the position as head of sales for an emerging organization. When I began my career, I was only the third salesperson to be hired, knew nothing of the industry, and had no relationships, but I was curious. I wanted to learn everything I could. Year after year, I accepted the challenges and opportunities that presented themselves. But I stayed comfortable, and nothing that presented itself felt beyond my capabilities. Nothing really stretched the boundaries for me. I advanced and achieved success, and then came a moment where I was presented with the opportunity I had been waiting for— the one I believed represented success for me. After 10 years of committing myself to learning the business and building relationships, I was offered the position of head of sales. It was a well-compensated opportunity, and I was the only woman in our company—a company now of nearly 500—to have worked through the ranks and to earn a spot on the executive team. I had put in the long hours and made the sacrifices, but up to this point I had not allowed myself to get out of my comfort zone yet. This was the defining moment when I had to muster the courage to believe in myself and to brave the unknown, the uncomfortable. And do you know what I did? I handed it back. I held it in my hands for a moment, convinced myself they had wildly overestimated my ability, and I declined the offer. And I let that opportunity go to a colleague—a gentleman who had taken almost the identical path as me, who had no greater knowledge or skill set than I did. But he did have the one thing I did not. He had the courage to take the chance. He had the courage to not be perfect yet, but be willing to accept the challenge to accomplish things, which he did not know, and a willingness to move forward anyway. Was this a gender trait? Is this something that men have more of than women? Or do women have a stronger propensity to fall into the perfection trap? Who knows? Something in me said, "Hold on! You can't go in there! You don't know everything you need to know yet. What if you trip, make mistakes, and you don't meet their expectations? You're too emotional, you're the peacemaker, not the dealmaker. You're not smart enough, tough enough, whatever enough. What about the people who believe you to be worthy? What if you let them down? You are not perfect yet." Do we as women, adopt a mentality that in order to succeed, we have to already have mastered something *before* we are even given the opportunity. Do we believe that men are not vulnerable? Have we adopted this sense that in order to compete in a male dominated world, that we can't show weakness?

I think part of the challenge that has shaped our thinking as women is in part a passive gender bias, which continues to affect women's ability to see themselves and be seen by others as leaders. Current workplace perceptions still favor traditionally masculine traits, such as determination, confidence, and decisiveness and penalize the perfection trap in a most insidious way. The rewards are given to those who will jump into the ring prepared or not. And needing to feel perfect, which may just have a gender bias, is not rewarded. When a woman shows masculine traits, she is often seen as aggressive and given harsh labels. I believe women themselves have adopted the limiting beliefs of the perfection trap in which we have to be accomplished before we allow ourselves to step into an advanced role. As a group we are less willing to be vulnerable for fear of being seen as weak and of attempting to stretch beyond our safe boundaries for fear of failing.

This brings up two vital questions: (1) As women, what belief systems are we addicted to that remain from the past? and (2) What if all our current limitations are self-imposed? How can we change the way we think to avoid these self-defined traps, which in turn will move the conversation towards something completely different? And there it is, that little question: *What If.* What if I had taken that position that I worked so hard for? What if I faced those fears of doubt and uncertainty head-on instead of worrying what would happen when it was found out I was not perfect? What if I had been mindful and authentic to my true capabilities, and surrounded myself with the people who believed in me? Could that have allowed me to jump into the ring without being perfect? What if I had taken on that challenge, using it as an opportunity for growth, with no certainty for outcome, and had the resilience to push in the face of adversity? More importantly, what if I had believed that what was great about me now, the imperfect me, would be the key itself to my success? What if I didn't have to conform to the persona or the skill set of the man that held the role before me?

So what if we actively change our thinking, whether it be a belief that we still face passive gender bias or if our limits are more self-imposed. What if we begin to consciously move into a generation that requires us to take ownership over how we see ourselves and lean into our inherent traits of passion, collaboration, guidance and support, and in doing so create that environment in which those things that are what make us amazing women, now make us great leaders!

Jerome Knyszewski published an article entitled "7 Characteristics of Hugely Successful Female Leaders."[4] In it, he describes seven characteristics extremely successful women have in common: they are confident, creative, humane and helpful, emotionally intelligent, they take purposeful action, they never give up, and they create a unique style. Not necessarily at all the same set of characteristics that you might use to describe successful men. They speak in part to the softer side of who we are as women, of self-awareness and transparency, of leaning in to the authenticity of ourselves.

Another 10 years passed until another opportunity presented itself. And for those 10 years I stayed in my comfort zone and moved in, out, and away from opportunities that would have stretched my limits, certainly my perceived limits. At a certain point, you realize this isn't enough, that you aren't willing to settle for your own comfort zone. I wasn't fulfilled. My curiosity was still there, but I was pushing it down. I yearned for growth and lamented those opportunities missed. I had done well, but I certainly was not where I truly wanted to be. I didn't feel accomplished. Then there it was again: A chance to take a step, a great big scary step. I was asked to head west, away from home and family and all that was familiar, to help lead an emerging health care technology company that was in the midst of transition. Although it was in my industry of focus, I had neither operations experience nor technology management experience. My inner demons rose up and sang that same familiar tune: "What could I possibly bring to the table?" But I was restless and unsatisfied. I knew if I didn't take this opportunity, I would never truly know what I was capable of. I could play it safe again, stay put, stay comfortable, but this time, the voice wasn't inside my head, it was inside my heart, and it told me to extend my reach and step into the unknown. So I did.

When I arrived, it was humbling. Actually, it's always humbling to be out of your comfort zone. In positions past, I could always do the actual work that I was there to oversee. But I wasn't schooled in computer science or writing code. I had profit and loss responsibility, yet my proficiency in reading and comprehending financial statements was limited. And for the first time ever, I felt the weight of 124 individuals who looked to me for leadership and a sense of stability. My confidence before had come from a sense of knowing: A safety that I could lead by doing. But not here, not now.

Brené Brown, a writer and research professor with whom I have come to find strength and connection, talks about how to attack challenging situations. Situations that leave you questioning whether you, as you are today, in all your imperfections, are good enough to handle. Her guidance is to get deliberate, get inspired, and get going.[5] So I began to focus on the aspects of the opportunity that were well within my control. I had a team that needed to be organized around a very specific set of tasks. I needed to quickly assess the skills on hand and the gaps that would keep us from performing. I needed to chart a course, and to provide the team with a sense of direction and purpose. All these things I could do. I could rely on my known traits, those of communication, of compassion, of decision making, and I could champion the team.

And suddenly my team had a voice. I was surrounded by amazing men and women who themselves had the courage of their own convictions. Day after day, I took the time to listen to their voices. To surround myself with those who complimented my gaps. And day after day, I gave my team all that I had, and I asked for all that I needed. I let them teach me as much as I guided them. I did it with authenticity, with knowing that I didn't need to be perfect in all aspects. I gave myself permission to be enough, and I used my fears and moments of uncertainty to remind myself that I didn't have to achieve perfection, I just needed to do my best. I reminded myself that by just acknowledging my imperfections others would open up to me and in making those connections, I could find support, and not the judgment of a false perfect. This part of my journey is still under way and the outcome remains unclear. Will I succeed? Who knows? But my curiosity, my self-awareness, and my desire grow will lead me through an incredible experience.

Along the way, I've realized that allowing myself to be curious means that sometimes I will be scared. It means that sometimes I might fail, and actually not worrying about the end, means that I can't really fail, I will always move forward, just sometimes in unanticipated ways. It means that sometimes doing something for me instead of making the action about someone else could make a difference. It means that I have changed my language from "how do I make them proud?" to "how do I improve myself?" Once I allowed that shift to occur, I could step actively into the unknown, with all its uncertainty. I could be vulnerable and embrace the experience without fearing the outcome would define me. And what if the journey defines me, not the destination?

As I was invited to join this amazing group of accomplished women, and participate in the development of a book that speaks to the challenges we've faced, and what we achieved in spite of those obstacles, I realize that I have come face-to-face with the very thing that was at the heart of my journey: fear, vulnerability, uncertainty, and the choice to open myself up and jump in, or to hide behind a shield of avoidance.

My little demons started to twist my beautiful *What If* question into a distasteful cocktail of fear. I could hear them in my mind: "What if I'm not worthy of telling a story that has any relevance to anyone?"; "What if my journey is not at all compelling?"; "What if my achievements don't come close to the other amazing women represented in this collection of stories?" What a terrible, fearful, unproductive way to think. So I stopped, silenced my internal demons, dug deep, and found the courage to be deliberate in my actions. And I wrote.

So to all of you who have chosen to read my words, here are the things that I hope you'll carry with you: Be mindful and authentic with your own journey, just as I strive to do in mine. Surround yourself with support, but be truly vulnerable and fully seen to those from whom you seek support, and always ask "What If." Choose curiosity over fear and continue to push towards that next amazing thing! The world is in constant motion and change is yours to grab as long as you choose. Change that we can't even imagine yet, but we can try and be curious and wonder *What If.*

Notes

1. S. Kipman, "15 Highly Successful People Who Failed on Their Way to Success." Lifehack.

2. Rachel Sugar, Richard Feloni, and Ashley Lutz, *Business Insider,* July 9, 2015. Retrieved from www.businessinsider.com/successful-people-who-failed-at-first-2015-7.

3. C. Craver, "The Impact of Gender on Bargaining Interactions," 2012. Retrieved from The Negotian Experts: http://www.negotiations.com/articles/gender-interaction/.

4. J. Knyszewski, "Professional Women," September 22, 2015. Retrieved from https://www.linkedin.com/pulse/7-characteristics-hugely-successful-female-leaders-jerome-knyszewski.

5. Brené Brown, "The Gifts of Imperfection." In The Gifts of Imperfection, edited by B. Brown, pp. 53–54. (Center City, MN: Hazelden Publishing, 2010).

Chapter 12

Game Changers

Artemis Emslie
CEO
myMatrixx

My story is not extraordinary. I am not extraordinary. I have learned, however, that ordinary people can do extraordinary things and exceptional leadership can come from unexpected beginnings with the right mentorship, the right attitude, and a lot of hard work.

Growing up in a two-bedroom apartment in a working-class neighborhood just north of Boston, I shared a room with my sister and my two brothers shared a converted porch. Those early close quarters contributed to the close-knit ties I still have with my family. We did not have a lot of "things," but we had a lot of love. I fondly remember family projects like making our own living room furniture so that we could have a place to sit together. My father built the framework, and the rest of us worked with my mother to fabricate the cushions and pillows. We used the furniture for many years, not only for its intended function; we also used the cushions and pillows for imaginative games when the weather was too cold to play outside.

Like all parents, mine wanted a better life for their children, and they impressed on us the importance of school, hard work, and family time . . . sometimes in unusual ways. My mother worked at the WIC (Women, Infants, and Children) office and would occasionally take us to work with her because she wanted to give us a strong visual sense of what true poverty was—and to motivate us to do whatever was necessary to create the kind of life she envisioned for us. She also frequently drove us through the most crime-ridden areas of town to give us an up-close view of the effects of illegal drugs. During these unconventional but highly educational tours, she would tell us, "This is your future if you don't go to college."

With my mom's encouragement, I entered the workforce at age nine when I got my first newspaper route. I spent my mornings before school on my bike throwing papers onto porches and driveways, and my weekends were spent collecting the $1.50 I had invested in the newspapers from the previous week. Always the optimist, each week I was hopeful for a tip or two, and I was always grateful when I got them. Between the paper route and babysitting, I got my first taste of entrepreneurship and the satisfaction of having a bit of my own money. This was my first game changer. When I was 14, I decided I was ready to take it to the next level. I lied about my age and landed a job at an ice cream parlor. I worked hard and after several years, I eventually earned enough money to buy my first car. It was a clunker, but it was my ride to independence.

My mother had two rules for college: (1) I had to study business and (2) the school I chose had to be far enough away from Boston that I could not come home on the weekends. Thanks to a cross-country scholarship and a small academic scholarship, I decided to study economics and headed 1,300 miles south to Weber College in Florida. My trusty old clunker, a diesel VW Rabbit, took me all the way there, but it didn't last long after that. The car had engine issues, and I had to "pop the clutch" to get it going. Ideally, I would park facing downward on a hill to make this process fairly easy. That worked in Massachusetts, but central Florida is completely flat, so I learned to be innovative. Being far away from home not only forced me to be independent but helped me hone my creative problem-solving skills. I learned to park far away from any other cars so that I could push start my car while running alongside it, and then hop in and be on my way. This was fantastic exercise and a great complement to the training I was doing with the track team!

After my first year of college, my clunker and I headed north to spend the summer with my family. Halfway through my journey home, I stopped at a rest area to use the restroom. I left my car running so that I would not have to struggle with starting it again. I was only gone a few minutes, but when I returned to the parking lot, I was shocked to see clouds of black smoke billowing out of my car. I will never forget the day my car blew up in Jessup, Maryland. Fun times.

My remaining college years were spent bumming rides from friends to get to school and work. Fortunately, I do not remember them ever trying to avoid me. Someone was always there lending me a helping hand, even when it was inconvenient. This experience was also game changing. I learned the value of modesty and the importance of altruism. To this day, I continually strive to keep these values at the forefront of who I am.

Another game changer happened when I was working as a bartender to support myself while I was finishing school. Attempting to launch a career in banking, the timing was not good because of the consolidating industry, and I was having trouble breaking into the industry. One night, two young men sat at the bar and starting talking about how much they loved their sales jobs. I overheard their lively conversation about fun and travel and money. It sounded glamorous, so I engaged them to find out more. When they told me they worked for a pharmacy benefit management (PBM) company, I had no idea what that meant, but I asked if their company was hiring. When they said yes, I asked for contact information to send a resume. They laughed and told me they were not hiring women.

Wait . . . what?

Momentarily stunned, yet fueled by a naturally competitive spirit, I was not letting that go. Game on, guys. I pushed for reasons and was told that women did not fit the company's profile for sales reps. Seriously. Discouraged but not deterred, I bided my time. After serving the men a couple more drinks, I pressed for contact information again and this time was successful. The next morning, I called the company and got the job. This was my first venture into a career in the PBM industry—an industry I had previously never even heard of. It was also an important lesson in the power of persistence.

Fast-forward a couple years. . . . Eager to advance my career, I decided it was time to look for a better opportunity, and I applied for a position with a drug manufacturer. During my fourth interview, I found out that there were hundreds of applicants for the position and I had made it to the final three candidates. When I got the call for a fifth and final interview, I was informed that the interview was set for 10 A.M. on a Friday. It was impossible for me to meet the hiring manager's schedule because of existing work commitments. There was no flexibility in the appointment, so with much reluctance, I had to decline the interview. However, I was not ready to give up on this opportunity. That Friday evening, without a detailed plan but armed with youthful confidence and naïve fearlessness, I drove 120 miles to the small town in New York where I knew the decision maker lived. My gut was telling me that I had to exhaust all efforts to get this job. The next morning, I went to a pay phone near a local diner, looked up the decision maker's home phone number, and asked him if I could get that final interview. Over breakfast, I landed the job.

As Teddy Roosevelt famously said, "Believe you can and you're halfway there."

My new sales job with the drug manufacturer presented many remarkable learning opportunities. I was assigned to cover the state of Connecticut. This was a new territory for the company, so it was my responsibility to introduce the company as well as their products. The sales training was exceptional and very beneficial. Because this was a new territory, there was no database of prospects to target. I spent a considerable amount of time going through the "yellow pages" to find doctor's offices. I quickly learned the times that I would most likely have an opportunity to get past the gatekeepers and speak directly to the doctors, even if only for a few seconds. This was another game changer. I was forced to greatly improve my organization and time management skills, and I became much more efficient. I loved the scrappiness that was required to be successful, and my entrepreneurial spirit was stoked again.

After proving my value, I was promoted to train new sales reps and relocated to Chicago. This was another opportunity to learn and grow, building new relationships and becoming skilled at the Midwestern way of doing business. A few years later, I was recruited by my former employer to move to Massachusetts and assume a management position. There, I developed a business plan to turn around the company's lagging business in Florida and Georgia. I negotiated a move back to Florida, where I turned the business around to the top-performing territory for the company. I gained valuable experience on both the workers' compensation and commercial sides of the industry before moving on to another company, where I took advantage of the opportunity to learn about another side of the business. This is where a met a truly wonderful mentor who took me under her wing and coached me on business acumen as well as the specifics of group health. Twenty years later, we are still close friends and are once again colleagues working on the same team.

Because of the opportunities that presented themselves, along with the opportunities I created for myself, by this time I was well-versed in many aspects of the health insurance business: managed care, the commercial third-party administrator (TPA) market, pharmacy benefit management, pharmaceutical sales, and health care plans. This set of experiences helped me stand out from others in my profession and propelled my career to greater heights. When I was pregnant with my first child, I was prepared to resign from my position, but when I made that difficult call to the CEO, I did not even get the words out before he told me that the company would strongly support work-family balance. With much help from my mother, I continued working and traveling extensively. Often, my mother and toddler would accompany me on road trips for a day or two on a moment's notice. (Thanks, Mom!)

Two years later when my second son was born, I had a new boss and lost the supportive workplace culture to which I had become accustomed. Without the flexibility and after one too many insensitive, chauvinistic comments, I left the company for a better opportunity in workers' comp. By now, I had developed a strong personal brand and expertise in various areas of the industry. I was again able to create my own opportunity by leveraging my knowledge of group health and transferring it to workers' comp to build new programs, develop new products, and to be successful in national sales. Unsolicited job offers were now coming my way. This was a pivotal point in my career and another game changer.

It was at this point that I decided to step outside of my comfort zone and pursue my entrepreneurial passions full time. I launched a successful auditing and consulting business to help payers make better buying decisions with pharmacy benefit managers. Hard work and confidence in my expertise paid off with contracts with blue-chip companies. After two years, however, I received an offer I could not refuse and left my consulting business to run a growing workers' comp PBM. When I was a child, I never dreamed that I would someday be the CEO of a multimillion-dollar company, but with tenacity, a strong foundation of support, and a bit of luck, here I am.

As I noted before, I have very modest roots. Although my parents struggled financially when I was a child, they understood the value of vacation time and always made family trips a priority. Whenever they had the gas money, we would pile in the car and get out of town. These mini vacations were usually only a day or two long but gave us time to connect as a family while exposing us to places outside of our neighborhood. My favorite trips were when we drove down to North Carolina to visit extended family. The stark contrasts between the urban culture of north Boston and the southern lifestyle of my cousins in Asheville always made these trips an adventure. It was during these visits that I began to develop an appreciation and respect for people's differences. These early experiences shaped who I am, and throughout my life, I have benefited so much by being open-minded and learning from others' perspectives and experiences.

Be humble. In order to be truly successful, it is essential to know what you don't know. In other words, recognize that no matter how talented or accomplished you may be, there are always people who have knowledge and special skill sets that you do not possess. One of the keys to success in my career has been to surround myself with talented people who fill in my gaps. In business and in life, each person you meet offers something of value . . . a fresh point of view, a special talent, a pearl of wisdom. Listen and learn from family, friends, colleagues, even strangers—and even when you disagree with them. There are always opportunities to learn and grow.

There are also opportunities to teach. One of the best things about leading a corporation is that it allows me to contribute to other organizations and give back to the industry that has nourished me and made me who I am today. From elevating the stature of women in our industry through the foundation of the Alliance of Women in Workers' Compensation to contributing to the Workers Compensation Research Group's (WCRI) valuable research, it is very gratifying to honor those who have helped me over the years by now paying it forward. The additional extracurricular pursuits of developing work-ready programs at my alma mater along with mentoring at-risk teenagers and budding entrepreneurs also keep me energized. My contributions in these arenas will ultimately be what I consider the pinnacle of my career. I know there is much more learning and growing ahead, and that is exciting.

The path to a successful career is a marathon, not a sprint. I have been fortunate to have had both good and bad experiences to learn from, as well as the opportunity to be mentored by several remarkable people. My journey began with going after opportunities that presented themselves early in my career. When I was in my 20s, I pursued the jobs that fortuitously came my way, usually without much thought. I let my intuition guide me to what seemed right at the time and I didn't worry about the qualifications. As my career progressed, I learned the value of strategic planning and creating my own opportunities within companies with new business plans that created value for the organization. Every step on my path presented a valuable experience for personal and professional growth.

Every person has his or her own definition of individual success. Mine has been balancing my family and my career. I did not always know where my career was headed, but I always knew I wanted to be a mom. I am from a large family, and as my two sons have reached their teenage years, I have developed a profound respect and admiration for my mother's skill of artfully balancing the demands of four children with a successful career. She was and still is my inspiration and my greatest role model.

It has been said that you can have it all—just not all at once. I think there is some validity to that statement. Just as my career was taking off, I knew the time was also right to start a family because "you're as young as you feel" does not apply in this situation. I was filled with trepidation over what is a very common concern for working mothers. Would I lose my edge if I put my career on pause to care full time for my children? Would I be able to provide the same value and pick up where I left off when I returned to the workforce? This internal struggle leads to a highly personal choice that so many woman have to make, and I understand and respect my friends' and colleagues' decisions to do what is best for themselves and their families.

Primarily driven by the desire to independently provide for my children if I ever needed to, my decision was to continue working after my sons were born. At this point in my career, I had considerable flexibility with my job but I also spent a great deal of time on the road. This presented challenges. Although I had to make some sacrifices, we made it work. As I watch my boys grow into caring, respectful young men, I do not regret my decision.

I have come to realize that success is constructed of many pieces. The foundation of my success was built by doggedness and luck of circumstance and strengthened by hard work. Asking questions, growing my knowledge base, and developing my professional skill set increased my value. Truly appreciating constructive criticism and learning from my mistakes added the next layer of success. Early in my career, my mother told me there would come a time when I would have options and would no longer ever have to worry about getting a job. Midway through my career, I knew I had achieved that level of success. This was another game changer. I had gained the confidence and competence to define and negotiate a new opportunity with a company that was a good cultural fit. My new role helped drive my career to greater heights. Each building block brought different opportunities for learning and solving problems. I discovered my entrepreneurial side and launched a successful auditing business that challenged me in ways I had never been challenged before. I pushed through the obstacles and the feeling of vulnerability that comes with starting a business and having no safety net. The risks are great, but so are the rewards.

My success has been cultivated through a passion for learning and an entrepreneurial spirit. Because of my track record, I found myself in the enviable position of simultaneously fielding unsolicited offers to lead three different firms. I ultimately chose to return to my passion for workers' comp and accepted my current post at Matrix Healthcare Services ("myMatrixx"). Navigating the growth curve and taking the company to the next level by focusing on what leads to business growth and profitability is very rewarding.

There is not one silver bullet that leads to success. My path to success has been a combination of many parts: the people who have shared their knowledge and guided me as well as those who have trusted me as a colleague and a partner; a strong desire to learn; the risks I have been willing to take; and hard work and determination. Most importantly, my success is fueled by a passion to make a positive difference by sharing what I have learned. I know that I am not better than the next person, but I am better because of the next person.

My advice? Trust your instincts. Know your value. Be bold. Take risks. And never stop learning.

Appendix

Women to Watch
(by year)

2015

Carrie Barr
Susan Bencher Daigle
Kristen M. Bessette
Teresa Black
Victoria Davison
Valerie DeMell
Artemis Emslie
Mary Forrest
Lindsey Frase
Rachael Ingle
Pam Kehaly
Linda Lane

Julie Layton
Florence Levy
Kristine Meuse
Donna Nadeau
Judi Newsam
Amanda Nguyen
Monica Ningen
Lynn Oldfield
Mary Beth Sanford
Kathleen Savio
Lori Seidenberg
Cara Tseng Duffield
Soraya Wright

2014

Jennifer Barton
Leah Binder
Beth Bombara
Jacqueline Day
Marialuisa Gallozzi
Dorothy Gjerdrum
Cary Grace
Tracie Grella
Donna Hodges
Anita Ingram
Amy Kessler
Joann M. Lytle
Carmen Ortiz-McGhee
Nicola Parton
Kathleen Reardon
Lindsay Rios
Tracy A. Ryan
Deborah Giss-Stalker

Kathryn Tazic
Iris Teo
Sherry Thomas
Karen Vines
Donna Vobornik
Kim Wilkerson
Tracy D. Williams

2013

Cory Anger
Sherri Bockhorst
Caroline J. Clouser
Noelle Codispoti
Yvette Connor
Marti Dickman
Angela R. Elbert
Marcela Flores
Lisa Freeman
Laura Greifenkamp
Sabrina Hart
Tracy Hatlestad
Susan Holliday
Diana Kiehl
Carolina Klint
Danielle Lisenbey
Christine Lithgow
Kathie Maley
Heather Masterson
Julie Mix McPeak
Kimberly M. Melvin
Colleen Reitan
Liliana Salazar
Jan E. Simonsen
Kimberly Waller

2012

Dr. Teresa Bartlett
Sara Bennett
Elizabeth D. Bierbower
Victoria Carter
Teresa W. Chan
Mildred Claire
Betty P. Coulter
Reshma Dalia
Janet Dell
Anna Engh
Jennifer J. Fahey
Ann Haugh
Dorothy E. Kelly
Karin Landry
Amy Laverock
Rocío Leal Pasarán
Selena J. Linde
Mandy McNeil
Deborah M. Minkoff
Roxanne Mitchell
Magdalena Nawloka
Janet Pane
Meredith Schnur
Peggy Scott
Maria Yao

2011

Marcia Benshoof
Libby Christman
Robin L. Cohen
Grace Crickette
Lori Daugherty

Michelle DuFour
Sharon Edwards
Laura Foggan
Mary Jane Fortin
Maureen Gallagher
Kimberly George
Sallie Giblin
Pam Humphrey
Toni Ianniello
Tina Y. Mallie
Kathleen R. McCann
Melissa Miller
Lisa Morgan
Karen O'Reilly
Terrie Pohjola
MaryAnn Sackman
Kristi Savacool
Cindy Slubowski
Kelly Superczynski
Caroline Woolley

2010

Eileen Auen
Jean Bisio
Valerie Butt
Melissa Carmichael
Jennifer R. Devery
Lisa Doherty
Alexis Faber
Grace Gandarilla
Elizabeth Haar
Letha E. Heaton
Jennifer Lunski
Debra McClenahan

Laurie Orchard
Sophia Phillip
Robyn Piper
Sheri Pixley
Carolyn H. Rosenberg
Chantel Sheaks
Cynthia R. Shoss
Caryn Siebert
Marguerite Soeteman-Reijnen
Kathryn Sullivan
Pattie Dale Tye
Alyson Warhurst
Maggie Westdale

2009

Jane Boisseau
Pamela R. Collins
Diane M. Davies
Dawn Dinkins
Lori Dickerson Fouché
Patricia Guinn
Patricia A. Henry
Jenny L. Housley
Ellen R. Kerr
Ingrid C. Lindberg
Deborah M. Luthi
Seraina Maag
Carol L. Murphy
Shari F. Natovitz
Jamie Ohl
Dawn Owens
Sarah Pacini
Louise Pennington
Carla Sans

Francine L. Semaya
Maria Sheffield
Carolyn Snow
Parul Stevens
Susan A. Stone
Martha Vinas

2008

Rebecca C. Amoroso
Diane Askwyth
Bonnie Boone
Alison Borland
Catherine Corrie
Susan Cross
Sarah Dalgarno
Christa Davies
Judy Gonsalves
Patricia Hemingway Hall
Ruth A. Hunt
Patricia Kagerer
Jacqueline Kosecoff
Diane Larrivee
Ann Longmore
LoriAnn Lowery
Holly Meidl
Martha Oakes
Jodi Prohofsky
Sharon Ritchey
Chelley Schaper
Mary Sklarski
Sheila Small
Katherine Smith-Dedrick
Peg Warner

2007*

Carol F. Arendall
Terri D. Austin
Dahna Baisley
Cynthia Beveridge
Raji Bhagavatula
Jennifer Boehm
Angela Braly
Linda Chase-Jenkins
Priya Cheria Huskins
Patricia A. Costante
Mary Craig Calkins
Elaine Caprio
Linda Dakin-Grimm
Carla D'Andre
Lisa Datelle Quarterman
Amy Flanagan
Michelle Futhey
Patricia Hagemann
Linda Havlin
Lisa Hawker
Teena Hostovich
Crystal V. Hover
Julianne Jessup
Cindy Keaveney
Ruth Kilduff
Linda D. Kornfeld
Rachel S. Kronowitz
Joan Lamm-Tennant
Danielle Lenzi
Melissa O. Leuck
Julie K. Long

Business Insurance named 80 Women to Watch honorees in 2006 and 50 honorees in 2007 to recognize those women who had a significant impact on the industry prior to the creation of the program.

Heidi Mack
Rebecca A. McLaughlan
Pamela Miller
Patricia A. Milligan
H. Elizabeth Mitchell
Brenda M. Olson
Stacey Regan
Pamela Ritz
Audrey M. Samers
Tamara Shelton
Gail Soja
Nancy Sylvester
Lauren Vail
Kate Van Hulzen
Sherron Williams
Lori Windolf Crispo
Kathryn Yates
JoAnne Ybarguen Dorsey
Carol A. N. Zacharias

2006*

Janice Abraham
Kathleen Angel
Tracey Ant
Nancy Aque
Wendy Baker
Brenda Ballard
Inga K. Beale
Jill B. Berkeley
Florence Bindelle
Mary S. Botkin

Business Insurance named 80 Women to Watch honorees in 2006 and 50 honorees in 2007 to recognize those women who had a significant impact on the industry prior to the creation of the program.

Deborah Broderick
Barbara C. Bufkin
Monica M. Burmeister
Kathleen M. Burns
M. Michele Burns
Pamela Carpenter
Karen M. Clark
Marsha A. Cohen
Christine Dandridge
Helen Darling
Pamela E. Davis
Elizabeth Francy Demaret
Carol Denzer
Marie Gemma Dequae
Corbette S. Doyle
Lynn Drennan
Alice Edwards
Karen K. Farris
Trish Getty
Alexandra Glickman
Connie Harden
Cathy A. Hauck
Barbara Haugen
Kathryn Hayley
Dr. Pamela A. Hymel
Karen Ignagni
Doris Johnson
Linda Johnson
Sharon Kaleta
Anastasia Kelly
Melissa Kerns
Joy Erven Laughery
Lou Ann Layton
Dierdre H. Littlefield
Fiona Luck
Eileen McCusker
Nancy M. Mellard

Susan R. Meltzer
Lara Mowery
Susanne Murray
Cecilia Norat
Lori S. Nugent
Leslie Nylund
Janice Ochenkowski
Susan J. Patschak
Mary Todd Peterson
Leigh Ann Pusey
Paula Rosput Reynolds
Pamela Rippens
Karen Rohan
Mary Roth
Joy A. Schwartzman
Lucille Sgaglione
Kelly Smith
Karen V. Sothern
Robin Sterneck
Kathleen Swendsen
Claudia P. Temple
Ellen Thrower
Karen Beldy Torborg
Sarah Turvill
Laurel A. Ulrich
Maxine E. Walker
Lisa Wall
Shelly Wolff
Kathy Woodliff
Millicent W. Workman
Lisa Zeitel
Liz Zlatkus
Marita Zuraitis

About the Authors

Carol Arendall
Vice President Safety & Risk Management
US Foods, Inc.

Carol Arendall spent close to 20 years at Saks Incorporated starting as an assistant risk manager, moving up to risk manager, and finally as the director of risk management for 14 years. At Saks, Carol was responsible for purchasing all the property and casualty insurance as well as claims management and service of process. Carol joined OfficeMax in 2005 as the director of risk management, responsible for the purchasing of all the property and casualty insurance, claims management, Bermuda-based captive and self-insured fronting programs, and legacy claims portfolio. Carol was also a leader of the enterprise risk management initiative at OfficeMax. In July 2009, Carol joined US Foods Inc. as their vice president of risk management. US Foods is one of America's largest food service distribution companies with 26,000 employees, 6,000 trucks, and more than 60 distribution centers across the country. US Foods distributes food and related products to more than 250,000 customers. Carol is responsible for purchasing insurance and claims management, as well as providing strategic direction on risk mitigation strategies throughout the company. Carol is part of the US Foods senior leadership group and is a part of the business risk committee. In 2015, Carol took on additional responsibilities leading the environmental health, safety, and security functions. Carol was a founding member of the advisory board for the National Retail and Restaurant Defense Association. She is also a board member of the Workers Compensation Research Institute, a charter member of Women Executives in Workers Compensation and a member of CLM (Claims Litigation Management Alliance). In addition, Carol was named to the *Business Insurance* 2007 Risk Manager of the Year® Honor Roll and named as one of 50 Women to Watch in the insurance industry 2007 by *Business Insurance*. Carol previously served WCAN and the National Workers Compensation Quality Council. She has served on the REBEX planning committee and has been a member of the Risk & Insurance Management Society for 25 years. She is a frequent speaker on risk management issues at various conferences across the country. She has a BS in business administration.

Yvette Connor
Managing Director
Insurance & Alvarez & Marsal Risk Advisory Services

Yvette Connor is a managing director with Alvarez & Marsal Insurance and Risk Advisory Services, with more than 20 years of experience building, quantifying, and testing operational, financial, hazard, and reputational risk frameworks. She is a thought leader on regulatory implications, including building and quantifying operational risk and effectively linking risk frameworks with governance platforms. Yvette focuses on identifying opportunities for value creation, including building decision-driven models informed by risk factors and organizational behavior. Her efforts help companies identify risk priorities and quantify impacts broadly throughout an organization or more narrowly by specific risk issue. Her soon-to-be-published thesis, entitled "Does Risk Management Matter to Shareholders," describes a methodology for risk management valuation and the effects of "good" risk management on organizational profitability and capital performance. Before that, Yvette served as the director of client engagement for

Marsh. Her primary focus involved leading a proprietary global servicing model to define clients' business needs and priorities, designing optimal risk management responses, and delivering value-add solutions alongside exemplary team performance. She helped to adapt the model for various global regions and clients, including training colleagues and leading a global communications effort. In addition, she was a member of the analytics sales team in the United States, supporting global risk management clients through the delivery of enhanced analytics. Prior to joining Marsh in 2010, Yvette was the director of risk management at Vulcan Inc., a privately held company with a diverse portfolio of over 200 operating companies. There, she led the development of a multidisciplinary risk management department that created an enterprise-wide risk management platform to identify and mitigate exposure to risk, while focusing on value for key stakeholders. Earlier, she served as vice president of risk management at Roll International, a global food producer, distributor, and product manufacturer, as well as director of insurance and risk financing at Sutter Health. Yvette earned an MS in risk management at New York University and an MBA in finance at the University of California, Davis. In 2013, *Business Insurance* magazine named her as one of the Women to Watch in Risk Management and Insurance, confirming her talents as a leader and innovator for risk management excellence. In 2008, *Treasury and Risk* magazine named her to their "40 under 40" list.

Artemis Emslie
CEO
myMatrixx

As CEO of myMatrixx, Artemis leads the strategic growth of the company's pharmacy business and its ancillary medical services program. With nearly 25 years of experience in both the workers' compensation and group health industries, Artemis brings a multidimensional perspective to the complex issues facing pharmacy benefit management clients. Prior to joining myMatrixx in 2012, Artemis held senior leadership positions with several companies, and then launched ProspeRx Solutions, a highly successful auditing firm for workers' compensation insurance providers where she provided pharmacy program review, Request for Proposal (RFP) management, vendor management and negotiation, and consulting services to several blue-chip clients. Artemis co-founded Alliance of Women in Workers' Compensation, a think tank committed to sharing ideas and mentoring tomorrow's industry leaders, and she currently serves on its advisory board. Artemis is chairperson of the Workers Compensation Research Institute Core Funders Group. She also serves on the advisory board of Kids' Chance, a nonprofit organization dedicated to providing scholarships for children of injured workers to help them achieve their educational goals. As a recognized industry expert, Artemis is a frequent speaker at national industry conferences on topics such as drug trends and best practices in pharmacy benefit management. In 2015, she was recognized as one of *Business Insurance*'s Women to Watch and was honored with WorkCompCentral's Comp Laude Leadership and President's Honor Roll awards. Artemis is currently working with the University of South Florida's College of Pharmacy faculty to develop an academic program that combines pharmacy doctoral education with business entrepreneurship.

Lindsey Frase
Executive Vice President
Willis Re, Inc.

Lindsey Frase is an executive vice president handling production and client account management for Willis Re in San Francisco. After starting her career at Guy Carpenter, Lindsey joined Willis Re in 2007, assisting in the formation of the Seattle branch office for reinsurance. Since joining Willis Re, the two-office Western Region has more than tripled brokerage revenue and is estimated to have the largest market share in the region versus all competitors. Lindsey is charged with running Willis Re North America's large-account property segment. At Willis, segments are the engines of business development within reinsurance. She is the global account executive for numerous key clients and works across customer type from global to regional companies. She's currently involved in the Willis Re client advocacy program as well as Willis's management development program. Lindsey was named a *Business Insurance* Women to Watch honoree in 2015. She also was involved in the formation of Women at Willis Northern California Chapter and the Insurance Industry Charitable Foundation's Women's Leadership initiative. She is a board member and treasurer of the Children's Health Guild charitable organization and a board member of the Educational Foundation of Orinda. Lindsey graduated summa cum laude with a degree in finance from Santa Clara University. Her graduating honors included the *Wall Street Journal* Award for outstanding student in finance and the Isabella Jones Prize for outstanding student in business. Lindsey has two sons, Liam, 5, and Aidan, 3. In her spare time, she enjoys skiing, golf, and hiking—with a goal of visiting every U.S. National Park in her lifetime.

Kimberly George
Senior Vice President, Corporate Development, M&A, and Health Care Advisor Sedgwick

With a unique history and depth of expertise, Kimberly George is frequently asked to share her insights on health care issues; business; and living a productive, meaningful life. Kimberly is an excellent speaker and a frequent presenter at national conferences and events. She is a highly regarded authority in the managed care and workers' compensation arena, and her work is regularly featured in industry journals and publications. Throughout her career, Kimberly has focused on creating health and productivity programs for employers, impacting quality care and cost of risk. She has been a registered nurse for 25 years, and although she began her career as a neuro-trauma nurse, she quickly transitioned to the insurance and benefits arena. Her experience in the field spans nearly 25 years and includes strategic planning, product development, benefit delivery models, and integrated disability management. Kimberly currently serves as senior vice president, corporate development, M&A, and health care at Sedgwick. In this role, she explores and works to improve Sedgwick's understanding of how health care reform affects its business models and product and service offerings. Kimberly previously served as Sedgwick's managed care leader. She joined Sedgwick in 2001 overseeing integrated disability medical programs and, later, leading Sedgwick's clinical operations, network solutions, and client relationships. Prior to joining Sedgwick,

Kimberly worked as a consultant in 24-hour health and managed care. She also held a leadership position with a large national managed care organization's case management division.

Carolina Klint
President
U.S. South Zone
American International Group Inc.

Carolina Klint was named president of the U.S. South Zone for AIG in March 2016. She is responsible for AIG's commercial business in Florida, North Carolina, South Carolina, Georgia, Tennessee, Alabama, Mississippi, Louisiana, Texas, Oklahoma, and Arkansas. Carolina joined AIG in 2003 and has held a number of positions of increasing responsibility within the organization. Most recently, she was president of the U.S. Southeast Zone, a position held since 2013. Before that, she was country general manager of AIG in Sweden. Under Carolina's leadership, AIG was named Insurance Company of the Year at the 2013 Insurance Awards held by *R&F,* Sweden's leading insurance publication. She has appeared on Swedish business weekly *Veckans Affarers'* list as one of "The 125 Most Powerful Women in Business" for three consecutive years and received the 2010 Business Supertalent Award. In 2013, Carolina was named a *Business Insurance* Women to Watch honoree. Carolina speaks frequently about values-based leadership, empowerment for breakthrough results, and the importance of diversity as a keynote speaker, panelist, and guest lecturer. She is a member of the board of directors of the Metro Atlanta Chamber, the board of trustees of the Georgia State University Risk Management Foundation, and the board of directors of Junior Achievement of Georgia. She resides in Dunwoody, just north of Atlanta, with her husband and their young son.

Linda Lane
President
Harbor Health Systems

Linda Lane is currently president of Harbor Health Systems, a leading provider of network effectiveness tools that identifies and selects the highest-quality providers to expedite treatment, recovery, and return to work for injured employees. Harbor Health is part of One Call Care Management (OCCM), the nation's leading provider of specialized cost-containment services to the workers' compensation industry, an organization she has been a part of since 1996. As a member of the executive leadership team, and throughout her career, Linda has played an active role in identifying and executing strategic changes necessary to shape the future vision and direction of the organization and sustain OCCM's growth. A graduate of Radford University with a bachelor's degree in business and management, Linda's industry and management expertise has been honed over her 20-year career in the workers' compensation arena working as executive vice president of business development, senior vice president of product strategy, and vice president of marketing. These achievements have provided her with a deep understanding of the issues facing the workers' compensations industry and the professional services solutions required to bridge regulatory requirements, manage cost drivers, and drive administrative efficiencies through technology. Her domain expertise has proven valuable internally and externally as clients, investors, and strategic partners look to develop forward-thinking claims and medical management solutions. In 2015, Linda was named a *Business Insurance* Women to Watch honoree.

Ingrid Lindberg
Chief Experience Officer
Chief Customer

Ingrid Lindberg is a serial customer experience officer. As one of the first CXOs in the country, she has been on the leading edge of customer experience for over 20 years. Her experiences have spanned the Fortune 500 across finance, health care, packaged goods, and retail, working with companies to create differentiating customer experience strategies and cultures. She's the chief experience officer at Chief Customer and helps companies turn theory into practice, building their customer experience and employee engagement strategies and making them actionable from customer service representatives to the

C suite. As CXO at Prime Therapeutics, Lindberg was responsible for developing and leading the implementation of their enterprise customer experience strategy. Her role within Prime was the first of its kind within the pharmacy benefit management industry. Her work led to Prime to a 21 percent increase in helpfulness of information and a 24 percent reduction to net effort. At the end of her time at Prime, members were reporting a 95 percent satisfaction and loyalty score—for the sixth consecutive quarter. Prior to joining Prime, Ingrid was the CXO at Cigna and was accountable for transforming the company into a consumer-centric brand. She was recognized for exemplary customer strategy development and received multiple awards for customer experience excellence. Her efforts led to a 156 percent improvement in customer understanding of benefits, a 50 percent reduction in the number of printed materials customers received, and the use of simpler language that didn't rely on health care jargon. The Words We Used is now the benchmark for health plan communications in America. Before her time at Cigna and Prime, Ingrid held roles with American Express, Pillsbury, Ceridian, SSgA, First Data, and Pier One, always working to enhance experiences for employees and customers. She was awarded a 2014 Maverick of the Year by the Stevie Awards for Women in Business for having significant impact on her industry. She also was awarded a 2014 Gold Stevie for the best new consumer product or service of the year for www.primehelps.com—a tool that simplified health plan selection for consumers. In 2013, she was named one of the Global 40 Under 40 in Marketing for her customer experience leadership and impact on the health care industry. In 2009, *Business Insurance* named Ingrid a Women to Watch honoree. She was awarded a Stevie award for customer communications in 2011 as well as a Gold CRM Award for implementation of her customer experience strategy by Gartner. Her work has been highlighted in an IBM Global Business Services case study called "Don't Yield on Customer Trust: Navigating the Customer Experience Journey on the Rough Road Ahead." Ingrid is an internationally recognized speaker and is heavily quoted by top publications including the *Wall Street Journal, New York Times, Atlanta Constitution Journal,* and *Kiplinger's.*

Carol L. Murphy
Managing Director
Aon Risk Solutions

Carol is Aon Risk Solutions' U.S. practice leader for casualty business development. She also leads Aon Risk Solutions' loss portfolio transactions practice and laser broking diagnostic platform. Previously, Carol served as Aon's central region practice leader, casualty broking, managing director and strategic account manager, and executive vice president and risk management practice leader at Aon Risk Solutions San Francisco. Prior to joining Aon, Carol started her career with Travelers and Johnson & Higgins. She has been a champion in Aon's global diversity and inclusion initiatives for more than 10 years and served as the leader of the Women's International Network for Aon both nationally and globally. Carol earned a BA degree from Bates College and her MBA from the University of Chicago, Booth Graduate School of Business. She has been recognized as a top "Power Broker" by *Risk & Insurance* magazine for eight years and as a "Responsibility Leader" in 2012 and 2015. Carol was honored as a *Business Insurance* Women to Watch honoree in 2009. She also was recognized as a "Woman Worth Watching" by *Diversity Journal,* and as one of the top 50 women in insurance by *Reactions* magazine in 2013.

Janet Pane
Head of Market Relationship Governance
Willis Towers Watson

Janet oversees the group strategy on market relationship governance as it relates to market derived income, and works in close alignment with the business leadership. In this role, Janet brings her unique combination of broker, compliance, and operational talents to the Willis Towers Watson leadership team. Janet started her career at Aon over 20 years ago on a production team where she learned the insurance brokerage business. Over the past 17 years, she has served in a wide variety of roles for the legacy Willis organization including director of global placement operations, director of client service, compliance director, chief operations officer, and sales and marketing director. Janet stays abreast of changes in our industry by serving on a number of industry panels and currently serves as chair on the board of directors for the Excess Lines Association of New York. An active promoter of diversity, Janet mentors a number of women in the industry and launched the workplace mentoring program with Big Brothers Big Sisters in the New York office. Janet leads the WTW client event for women at the Risk & Insurance Management Society's annual conference and has been recognized for her leadership and support of women in the insurance industry by the National Association of Insurance Women in 2011 and *Business Insurance*'s Women to Watch in 2013. Janet graduated with a degree in performing arts from New York's American Musical and Dramatic Academy and enjoyed touring the world with professional theater companies until a career in insurance took center stage. Janet lives at the Jersey shore with her husband and two teenage daughters.

Terrie Pohjola
Board Member
Thrivent Trust Company

Terrie Pohjola is a CPA with more than 25 years of experience serving on for-profit, nonprofit, and trade association boards. Terrie currently serves on the board of directors at Thrivent Trust Company, where she chairs the audit committee. Thrivent Trust Company is a wholly owned subsidiary of Thrivent Financial, a Fortune 500 financial services organization. She previously served on the Thrivent Financial Bank Board. Terrie also has previous experience on several nonprofit boards including United Way Fox Cities, serving as board chair and vice chair; Big Brothers Big Sisters of the Fox Valley Region; Gordon Bubolz Nature Preserve; Information Technology Association of Wisconsin; Property Casualty Insurance Association of America; Youth Services of the Fox Valley (now Boys & Girls Club); and the St. Elizabeth Hospital Community Foundation. Terrie recently retired from SECURA Insurance, where she served in a variety of executive leadership positions in information technology, sales, and finance, including corporate treasurer. Previous to joining SECURA, she spent 15 years in officer-level positions in the banking industry. Terrie holds a BS in managerial accounting and an MS in environmental economics from the University of Wisconsin Green Bay. In 2011, Terrie was named a *Business Insurance* Women to Watch honoree, and in 2013 she was recognized as a Director to Watch by *Directors and Boards* magazine.

Caryn Siebert
Vice President and Chief Claims Officer
Knight Insurance Group

Caryn is vice president and chief claims officer of Knight Insurance, part of the Hankey Group. She has been a contributor and leader in the insurance industry for many years and was twice a finalist for the CLM Claims Professional of the Year. Caryn has dedicated her career to building high-performance teams and striving for operational excellence as a senior executive with several diversified insurance companies and service entities. She was a finalist for the E&Y Entrepreneur of the Year Award–Orange County in 2013 and on the 2010 *Business Insurance* list of Women to Watch. She received the Kids Konnected 2008 Ambassador to the Children Award. At Knight, Caryn leads the claims operations including oversight of third-party administrators across the country and internal teams of claims professionals. Knight, on the Inc5000 list of fastest-growing companies in 2013, 2014, and 2015, provides capital support to profitable niche program business, on an admitted and nonadmitted basis. Knight is open for submissions from all sources and focuses on well-conceived and well-managed niche programs in the areas of commercial auto, general liability, professional lines, financial guaranty, and other specialty areas. Delivering results through relentless execution, Caryn's team focuses on quality products, excellence in customer service, and proactive risk management. She has been the public voice of claims and related issues for the company, while leading internally through example and influence, establishing organizational identity through open communication, honesty, and passion. Under her guidance, Carl Warren & Company made the 2014 Inc5000 list of fastest-growing private companies and was awarded the National ESOP Company of the Year for 2013. Prior to Carl Warren, Caryn was vice president/claims director of Safeco Insurance in Washington. She was part of a leadership team that over-hauled the claims operation. Prior to that, Caryn was director of com-mercial claims for GE Employers Reinsurance in Kansas and before that, senior vice president of Customer Operations/General Counsel for GE Coregis in Illinois. Preceding that, Caryn served as general counsel for Crum & Foster in New Jersey. She began her career in 1986 as an associate with LeBoeuf, Lamb in New York. She graduated cum laude from New York Law School where she was a law journal editor. Caryn has authored numerous industry publications, is a fre-quent speaker at RIMS, PRIMA, NRRDA, CLM and MC-CD, cur-rently chairs the Combined Claims Conference, and sits on the board of Kids Konnected.

Index